The Repairer of the Breach

Returning to Our Heavenly Father

Don Smith

Strategic Book Publishing and Rights Co.

Strategic Book Publishing and Rights Co., LLC
USA | Singapore
www.sbpra.net

For information about special discounts for bulk purchases, please contact Strategic Book Publishing and Rights Co., LLC Special Sales, at bookorder@sbpra.net.

ISBN: 978-1-950015-82-5

Table of Contents

Acknowledgements

I have so many people to thank that I am concerned that I might miss someone. To my parents, thank you from the depths of my heart for being wonderful parents, wonderful examples, who raised me in the respect and admonition of the Lord. To my father, though you are gone and await the return of our Lord and Savior, Jesus Christ, I see you daily when I look in the mirror and when I look at my son. Thanks for so many life lessons, especially the one where you told me "Son, if you want to know what the road is like up ahead, ask the man coming back." My father knew what networking and connecting with people was way before those terms became popular in the culture in which we live. To my mother, thank you for listening to the voice of God and instructing me in the way that He told you. I continue to run daily, Mom, trying to fulfill what the Father and you have told me. You have always been blessed by God with the ability to speak the right word at the right time. My love for you and Dad can never be measured in words. I love you very much!

To Robin, for loving me unconditionally, for standing by me when it appeared all had left, for encouraging me to rise to God's call and "shine" and for assisting the heavenly Father in making me the man I am today. Words fall short, and they pale in significance when I endeavor to express what you have done for me and the rewards that await you at the "bema."

To Rev. Mark Wallace—Mark, thank you for teaching me how to minister to God's people. Your example will always be in my mind. Your love for God's people, your boldness, your loving heart, and your ministry have refreshed me and given me courage to move forward with the things of God. You have been an edifying machine in my life and a great source of inspiration to carry out God's will. Thank you for seeing the Christ in me and helping me to develop it without pretense. You have seen the Christ in me and have been willing to pour out your life to me to help me develop to my fullest potential, all the while honoring my freedom to be who God made me to be. Your words, life, ministry, and encouragement have been a catalyst for this project. Thank you. I love you!

To Ron Wright, the word of God declares in Proverbs 27:17: "*Iron sharpeneth iron; so a man sharpeneth the countenance of his friend.*" You have always sharpened me with your boldness and open candor. Many who know us have often described our friendship as one of a covenant, like the one between David and Jonathan. You are truly my brother from a different mother, but we have the same heavenly Father. Thanks for your love, believing in me, and helping me to see that my life and ministry is even bigger than I ever thought or dreamed.

To my editor, Claudettee Royal, thanks for allowing my heart and words to remain in their original context so that my voice may be heard by those who have ears to hear. Your work and efforts are deeply appreciated. I know that the Father will reward you abundantly for your heart of service.

To anyone else I may have forgotten to mention, charge it to my head and not to my heart. May the word of God that God has allowed me the privilege to comprehend, understand, and teach edify you all and move you toward your fulfillment and repair any breach in your walk with the heavenly Father. You are all loved and appreciated by me!

Introduction

Isaiah 58:12:
And they that shall be of thee shall build the old waste places: thou shalt raise up the foundations of many generations; and thou shalt be called, The repairer of the breach, The restorer of paths to dwell in.

God, in His infinite wisdom and foreknowledge, made every necessary preparation for man and woman. God knew man would fall from the lofty state that He put him in. Therefore, God knew man would need a redeemer. God also knew that during certain time periods and generations, the accurate knowledge of His word would be hidden and shrouded by the devil through religion and legalism, and that His word would need to be rediscovered. God knew that the foundations of life for generations to come would periodically need to be reestablished. God knew that man would lose his way and form a breach. Hence, He promised in the Old Testament, here in Isaiah, that He would not leave Himself without a witness, and He would bring up men and women who would lift up God's standards, who would partner with God, our heavenly Father, to repair the breach and restore the paths of life that God desired men to walk in.

God, via the prophet Isaiah, confronts His people the nation of Israel in this fifty-eighth chapter. God opens by declaring to Isaiah to "Cry aloud, spare not, lift up thy voice like a trumpet, and shew my people their transgression …" (Isaiah 58:1). God informs us that though Israel has transgressed and sinned, they act as if they have done no wrong. Israel continues to approach God daily. They continue to want to know God's ways, to act as if they are a righteous nation, who never forsook the ordinances of God, and they take great delight in approaching God (Isaiah 58:2).

What a revealing look into the minds and hearts of the people of God at this particular time period. It is revealing because it fits so well today. Many of God's people today enjoy religious ritual and legalism. They enjoy "approaching" God, going through some type of religious practice that they think brings them closer to God. Many born-again Christians are substituting religious activity for a true and vital relationship with the Father, just like Israel did.

One of Israel's religious activities is spoken of in this chapter: fasting. God pulls back the veil and shows Israel their motives for fasting are religiously impure. Because of that, they are unable to be what God truly wants them to be. Notice that it is not the act of fasting that is the problem, but the motive of heart behind the fasting. God reveals that Israel fasted for "strife and debate … to make your voice be heard on high" (Isaiah 58:4).

Our wonderful God made a way for Israel to escape the religious trap they were in by revealing to them the *true* fast that He desired then and still desires in our day and time. In Isaiah 58:5, God told Israel that He never desired a fast to be a day where a man afflicts his soul, bows his head as a bulrush, or spreads sackcloth and ashes under him. This kind of fast is not an acceptable day unto the Lord. An acceptable fast to God, according to Isaiah 58:6-7, is to lose the bands of wickedness, to undo heavy burdens, let the oppressed go free, to break every yoke, to deal thy bread to the hungry, to bring the poor that are cast out to thy home, and to cover the naked. In other words, the *true* fast of God is a lifestyle of service to your fellow man. In fact, when the Messiah of Israel came on the scene and began bringing great deliverance to people and was questioned how he did it, Jesus Christ declared "by prayer and fasting" (Matthew 17:21).

God never desired religion or ritual. He wanted His people to have a true and vital relationship with Him and live a lifestyle of service to their fellow man, which in turn would bring them great salvation and deliverance. It is not the lifestyle of denying myself food and water that will truly deliver people, but a lifestyle of service, a lifestyle of spiritual impartation to others, a lifestyle of loosening the bands of wickedness, undoing heavy burdens, letting the oppressed go free, etc.

Jesus Christ spoke of this fast again in Luke 4:18-19:

The Spirit of the Lord is upon me, because he hath anointed me to preach the gospel to the poor; he hath sent me to heal the brokenhearted, to preach deliverance to the captives, and recovering of sight to the blind, to set at liberty them that are bruised, to preach the acceptable year of the Lord.

Now, back to the book of Isaiah. Look what God says happens to the individual who engages in the *true* fast of God in Isaiah 58:8-12:

Then shall thy light break forth as the morning, and thine health shall spring forth speedily: and thy righteousness shall go before thee; the glory of the Lord shall be thy reward.

Then shalt thou call, and the Lord shall answer; thou shalt cry, and he shall say, Here I am. If thou take away from the midst of thee the yoke, the putting forth of the finger, speaking vanity;

And if thou draw out thy soul to the hungry, and satisfy the afflicted soul; then shall thy light rise in obscurity, and thy darkness be as the noon day:

And the Lord shall guide thee continually, and satisfy thy soul in drought, and make fat thy bones: and thou shalt be like a watered garden, and like a spring of water, whose waters fail not.

And they that shall be of thee shall build the old waste places: thou shalt raise up the foundations of many generations; and thou shalt be called, The repairer of the breach, The restorer of paths to dwell in.

"Wow!" I want to shout. Look at the benefits of the *true* fast of God (a lifestyle of service). Your health will spring forth, God will protect your rear or back side (rereward) with His glory. You can call God and He will answer. In times of trouble or obscurity, our light, which is God Himself, will arise. The Lord will continually guide us. Look at the benefits God makes available.

This book, *The Repairer of the Breach*, is my contribution to raise up the foundations of God for my generation and those to come. It is my effort to help God's people repair any breach between themselves and the Father, and to restore paths for men and women of various backgrounds, cultures, and races to walk or dwell in.

In chapter one, "The Goodness of God," you will learn that God "is only good always." You will see that God is not the author of death, destruction, chaos, and confusion. It is the adversary who is the author of death. Armed with this knowledge, you will be able to stand against the adversary in your life. In chapter two, "God is Our Sufficiency, Fear Not," you will see it is never God's will that you have fear in your life, and it shows how you can eliminate fear by trusting God and making Him your sufficiency in all things. In chapter three, "Keys to Overcoming Challenges," you will learn that challenges are a part of life, but God has given us the keys to overcome any challenge that may arise. In chapter four, "Character of God," you will see that our God has character, and you will see eight aspects of His character (though there are many others). Learning and understanding the character of God will help you love Him more and remain faithful to Him. In chapter five, "Freedom in Christ," you will see that you have been made free in Christ Jesus and how it is *not* the will of the Father that you be in bondage to anything, including religious legalism. In chapter six, "Overcoming to Reach the Goal," you will see that God has called you to a unique lifestyle and how the adversary can use the senses realm to impede you from reaching your goals. But as we overcome "the sin," we will be victorious and reach our goal(s) in life. You will see what Apostle Peter had to overcome in order to carry out the calling or instructions of Jesus Christ. In chapter seven, "Reflecting Him: Excellence," you will learn of the excellence of God and how His children should reflect His excellence in their daily living. You will see how we bring God's excellence to pass based on a thought-confession-action link. In chapter eight, "God's Healing Wholeness," you will learn that healing is a large part of God's nature, that healing is more than physical, that believing is required for healing, and that as disciples of the Lord Jesus Christ we have been authorized to bring God's healing to our communities. Then in chapters nine and ten, "Love of God," you will learn the power of God's love, what love is, and how love is not based on a walk of convenience. You will also learn how to walk greater in the love of God, as we study the life of the one who is the epitome of God's love, the Lord Jesus Christ.

May God bless you, and may you join me in helping our generation and generations to come walk and live in the fullness of God as we become *The Repairers of the Breach*.

Chapter One

The Goodness of God

God is only good always. The devil is only evil always.

Few people truly believe the above statement. Many people in this walk of life do not believe in God or the devil. Then there are those who believe that there is a God and there is a devil, but they lack the knowledge and truth regarding the nature of the true God and the nature of the devil, the adversary. Hence, God is often blamed for the evil that occurs in this world. God is blamed for death, destruction, sorrow, and a whole host of other things. I will show you from the integrity of God's word (the Bible) that God is only *good* and is not the cause or source of evil in the world or in our personal lives.

In whom the god of this world hath blinded the minds of them which believe not, lest the light of the glorious gospel of Christ, who is the image of God, should shine unto them." (2 Corinthians 4:3-4)

The Bible declares there are only two gods, one is the God and Father of our Lord Jesus Christ, and the other is the "god of this world," the devil. The devil became the god of this world when he tempted Eve in the garden of Eden. The devil caused Adam and Eve to commit treason against the true God. By doing so, the devil was able to usurp the power of the delegated position and authority of Adam, who had dominion until he sinned against God. The devil, as the god of this world, has blinded people's minds. Therefore, they now have a contaminated view and perspective on the one true God. The adversary does everything he can to taint, hide, and cover God's true nature. He will even use people to accomplish his purposes. Unfortunately, many times, those he uses are religious people, so-called men and women of God. How many times have you heard people say that God called so and so "home to heaven"? How many times have you heard religious people use God's name to explain away death and destruction? These people are well-meaning, but that does not guarantee that what they speak is the truth. God's word is truth—period. Jesus Christ declared this in John 17:17 when he said: *"Sanctify them through thy truth; thy word is truth."*

If I want to know the *truth*, I must go to God's word. If I want so-called facts and opinions of men, all I need to do is listen to someone talk, watch the news on TV, or read a magazine or newspaper. But if I am after *truth*, there is only one place, one source for me to go to, and that is God and His Word.

The secret to the devil's success is his ability to convince people that he does not exist. Thereby, people blame the one true God for everything. If the devil does not exist, or I lack knowledge from the word of God about the true nature and function of the devil, then I will naturally blame

God for everything that occurs in this world, both good and evil. As you listen to people talk, you may hear them blame God or say that God is the source/cause of death, car accidents, natural disasters (which they now call "acts of God"), sickness, and a list of other evil things. This just can't be true, because the word of God fully contradicts this mindset regarding our heavenly Father.

Most people fail to comprehend that the Bible is an Eastern book, written by men of God who lived in an Eastern culture that is drastically different from our Western culture. The Eastern culture's use of language is often perplexing to the Western mind. Many of the so-called contradictions in the Bible are related to the reader's lack of knowledge around the Eastern culture, its language, and its use of figures of speech. I, like so many in today's world, thought and believed that God killed people and did other ghastly things for disobeying Him. I was blessed when I learned that this was not true and that I needed to understand the figure of speech in the Bible called an idiom. An idiom is a colloquialism, a way of speaking that can't be taken as literal or understood from words alone.

The great biblical scholar E. W. Bullinger notes in his book, *Figures of Speech Used in the Bible*, that the Hebrew language has an idiom of permission, and this idiom is used "to express, not the doing of the thing, but the permission of the thing which the agent is said to use." The idiom of permission must be understood in the light of God, creating man with free will. God didn't create mankind as pre-programmed robots. God, in His loving nature, created man with free will. God cannot and will never violate that free will. Hence, by His very nature and the law He established,

God permits man to make free-will choices that bring good or evil into his life.

It says in Exodus 10:20: "*But the Lord hardened Pharaoh's heart.*" This means God allowed or permitted Pharaoh's heart to be hardened by Pharaoh's own free-will choice. This verse is an example of the idiom of permission. Once Pharaoh went in a certain direction, God had to allow it. Otherwise, God would have had to override Pharaoh's free will, and God never does that. When we refuse to do or live God's Word and decide to turn away from God, we step outside of His protection. Mankind brings evil upon themselves when, due to a free-will choice, they turn away from God.

I form the light, and create darkness: I make peace, and create evil; I the Lord do all these things. (Isaiah 45:7)

Now, this verse appears to contradict everything I have said up to this point, but if we just think, we see there is no contradiction. I already said that God has created all men with free will, but how can there be free-will choice if there is not more than one option? By God creating light, he naturally created the potential for darkness. By God creating *goodness*, He created the potential for *evil*. If there were no choices other than what God commands, then man would not actually have free will. Choice always implies more than one option. There is no variableness in God's will and purpose for man—the variableness *always* lies in man's response to God's Word.

This can be clearly seen in the record of Noah and the flood. People say, "Well, God killed all those people in the days of Noah." No, He did not. You know who killed those people? The devil killed them. The people were complicit in their own death and destruction by violating God's Word. God warned the people in Noah's day that a flood was coming. God's warning was a demonstration of His *goodness*. The people, by free-will choice, decided not to obey God's commands via Noah, who preached or taught God's righteous standards (2 Peter 2:5), and therefore suffered the consequences of their failure to obey. God did not kill them. They could have all been saved.

This principle is seen throughout the word of God, in records like the people in Sodom and Gomorrah, and Pharaoh and the Egyptians, and it will bear out in our day with the return of Jesus Christ. Man has free will. He can use that free will to worship and respect God. Since the beginning of time, this has always been available. When man chooses God and His Word, blessings ensue, but if he chooses not to love God and obey His Word, this leaves the door open and gives the adversary access to his life.

Look at John 10:10: "*The thief cometh not, but for to steal, and to kill, and to destroy: I am come that they might have life, and that they might have it more abundantly.*"

Jesus Christ uses figurative language in this verse to describe the adversary, the devil. Jesus Christ calls the adversary "the thief." Is our heavenly Father a thief? Absolutely not, but the devil is! Not only is he a thief, but Jesus Christ lays out for us the three main objectives of the adversary, which is to steal, kill, and destroy. Every time the adversary shows up or is given access to a person's life, he is coming only to do one or a combination of three things: steal, kill, and destroy. The adversary comes to steal your health via sickness and disease; sickness and disease are not of our heavenly Father. The adversary comes to steal your convictions of life. He comes to steal your motivation and commitment to the heavenly Father. He comes to steal your knowledge of the word of God. Not only does he come to steal, but he comes to kill. This verse says that the devil is the one that kills, not our heavenly Father. Then, last but not least, the adversary comes to destroy. In E. W. Bullinger's *Critical Lexicon and Concordance to the English and Greek New Testament*, the word *destroy* is defined as "to ruin or have loss" (not annihilation). What great learning from this one verse. If the devil can't steal or kill, he will destroy; he will bring ruin or loss to people and nations.

However, in stark contrast to the three objectives of the adversary, Jesus Christ makes it clear that the purpose of his coming is to provide mankind with a life which is more than abundant! Who sent Jesus Christ? Whose words did Jesus Christ speak? Who did Jesus Christ represent on earth? Whose will did Jesus Christ say he always did? (John 5:30) The answer to all of these questions is God, our and his heavenly Father. Therefore, in John 10:10, we clearly see the nature of the devil (steal, kill, and destroy) and we see the nature of our heavenly Father (to give life and to give it more than abundantly). That's right. God wants you and me to have a life that is more abundant. He wants you to have and experience abundance in every category of life—spiritually, physically, materially, and financially. Why? Because God is *only good always!*

There is not one ounce of evil or darkness in our heavenly Father. If God caused evil, then evil would have to be a part of His makeup, His nature. What has confused people on this subject is not distinguishing the difference between God the creator and God the heavenly Father. God is the creator of all men, but he is *not* the Father of all men. I am a father of two wonderful children. I am accountable and responsible for their lives. Why? Because they are my children; I fathered them. What about God? God made, formed, and created the first man, Adam, but He has not fathered all men. In order for God to be your Father, you must believe unto salvation and be born again. You must receive Holy Spirit, God's gift. The how of the new birth is found in Romans 10:9. A man or woman must confess with their mouth that Jesus is Lord and then believe in their heart that God raised Jesus from the dead. Until a man or woman does this, God is not their heavenly Father and ultimately is not obligated to protect their lives.

This then is the message which we have heard of him, and declare unto you, that God is light, and in him is no darkness at all. (1 John 1:5)

God would not be only good if there was darkness in Him. This point of truth is so difficult for people to understand, due to years of exposure to wrong teaching (false doctrine) on this subject matter. God is light, and there is no darkness in our heavenly Father. This truth is a central truth to the entire word of God that must be understood if man is going to walk with the Father and live a life that is more than abundant.

Every good gift and every perfect gift is from above, and cometh down from the Father of lights, with whom is no variableness, neither shadow of turning. (James 1:17)

Is death a good gift? Is death a perfect gift? Is being poverty stricken a good and perfect gift? Is having cancer or any other disease a good and perfect gift? I say no! Therefore, these things can't be of God our Father. These things must come from another source. They must come from the god of this world, the devil. Notice the word *variableness*. It is defined in Bullinger's *Lexicon* as "a passing from side to side, a variation." Ever meet a person who is moody? One minute they are happy, the next they are angry? One day they wake up on one side of the bed, the next day the other side. Our God is not like that. He does not love one moment and then hate the next. He does not save your life one day and then kill you the next. Synonyms for variableness are: changeable, wavering, fickle, unsteady, unstable, uncertainty. None of these words describe our heavenly Father. Every good and perfect gift comes from Him, with whom there is no fickleness, wavering, or unsteadiness. Why? Because God is *only good always*. What a heavenly Father, what a God to love and trust!

I had fainted, unless I had believed to see the GOODNESS of the Lord in the land of the living. (Psalms 27:13)

Look at David's words. He says he would have fainted, caved in, given up unless he had believed to see, to physically see with his eyes the goodness of the Lord. For David, the *goodness* of the Lord was seeing the manifestation of the promise of God come to pass in his life. David believed and saw joy, love, prosperity, and wholeness in his life. This is what kept him going in the rough times of his life because he knew that the God he served was full of *goodness*. Notice, David did not believe to see wrath, division, poverty, sickness, etc. Why? He knew none of those things were of God, so he believed to see God's *goodness*. What should you believe to see in your life? God's *goodness*! If we don't see God's *goodness* in our lives, we will all be tempted, like David, to faint.

Years ago, my family and I decided to move to another state. I had been offered a great-paying job with the possibility for upward mobility. Well, after about eight months at the new job, I learned it was not what I expected or was led to believe. I was faced with a choice: pack up and move back to my home state, or stick it out. The decision was made to stick it out. Hence, I resigned from this particular employer and moved to another city within the same state. My wife was quickly able to locate employment, but I was not. I tried to find work that would allow me to work in my field (criminal justice) but was unable to do so. The economic pressure mounted quickly, and I had to take whatever employment I could find. So, a friend of mine hired me on his drywall crew. I helped to hang drywall for about nine dollars per hour. This job helped, but by no means did it cause the economic pressure to subside.

During my Christian walk, I have been one to tithe. Now, due to circumstances, I was tempted not to. I had discussions with myself like, "God will understand if I stop tithing for a while. I can't even make ends meet. I need to keep my tithe to help my family." So, with encouragement from other Christian believers, I made the decision to trust God and stand on His Word regarding the tithe. I kept tithing and even increased my giving over and above the ten percent. I did not do this for just a few weeks, but I stood faithfully on God's promises regarding tithing and prosperity until the manifestation of what He promised came to pass.

You should also be aware that during this time period our family was without any insurance. Just one accident could have taken us out financially. But guess what God did for me and my family during this critical time? I was able to gain new employment, not once but three times over about an eighteen-month span. Each new employment opportunity came with a pay increase better than the previous job. Not only did I increase my pay, but not a single family member had as much as a cold or a hangnail during that time period. God protected my family and rebuked the hand of the enemy, as He promised He would do in the book of Malachi (Malachi 3:10-12). I made the choice to tithe and God's blessings ensued. Why? Because *God is only good always!*

Now, let us look deeper into the goodness of God by taking a look at more scriptures related to that.

And the Lord descended in the cloud, and stood with him there, and proclaimed the name of the Lord. And the Lord passed by before him and proclaimed, The Lord, The Lord God, merciful and gracious, longsuffering, and ABUNDANT in GOODNESS and TRUTH. (Exodus 34:5-6)

Here, God declares of Himself to Moses that He is "abundant in goodness and truth."

He loveth righteousness and judgment; the earth is full of the

GOODNESS of the Lord. (Psalms 33:5)

It may be difficult for you to believe this truth, especially if your focus is the five o'clock news. What we focus on determines whether we see the *goodness* of God. We must focus on God's Word in order to see God's *goodness*. You will never see God's *goodness* if your focus is on the senses realm and what it produces. The news, TV, and magazines are often used by the god of this world to taint us, make us negative, and impact our focus so that we rarely see the beauty and *goodness* of God.

For the Lord God is a sun and shield: the Lord will give grace and glory: no GOOD thing will he withhold from them that walk uprightly. (Psalms 84:11)

What sane parent withholds good things from their children when it is possible to provide them? You wouldn't, so what about God? Are you a better parent than God? I don't think so. Our believing walk and lifestyle determines what the Father can provide for us. If we walk uprightly, which simply means to live God's Word, then He will hold no good thing from us. Not only will He give us good, but He also wants to give and share His grace and glory with us. Grace is God's unmerited favor. Unmerited means receiving something you don't deserve or did not earn. God wants to provide His children with His favor, but that's not all. He also wants to share His glory with us. Glory is brilliance, that which attracts attention or commands recognition. It can also be defined as manifested power. I'm ready to leap out of my seat! Imagine that—the God of heaven wants to give me goodness, His favor, and allow me to have His glory, His manifested power. Can you see why I keep saying our heavenly Father is only good always? What a God we have!

Oh, how great is thy GOODNESS, which thou hast laid up for them that fear thee; which thou hast wrought for them that trust in thee before the sons of men. (Psalms 31:19)

David tells us that God's *goodness* is laid up for those that fear (reverence, respect) God. You reverence and respect God by reverencing and respecting His written Word. If we do that, God's *goodness* is laid up for us. If I was a millionaire, I would have no problem going to my financial institution and making a withdrawal of more than $2.50. Why? Because I know my money is there, laid up for me. So why, as a son or daughter of God, would I not go before the throne of God (Hebrews 4:16) and make withdrawals on the *goodness* of God that is laid up for me? But most of us don't do this, and you know why? David explains in Psalms that I can't tap the resources of God without loving and trusting Him. The *goodness* of God is laid up for those of us who revere Him and trust him with our whole heart.

The god of this world is the source of evil because he is *only evil always*. In contrast, our wonderful God and heavenly Father is the source of all that is *good* and perfect, because he is *only good always*. He has laid up His goodness for us that love and trust Him. He wants to share His favor, which we have not earned and do not deserve. He wants us to manifest His glory, His power, and He promises not to withhold anything *good* from us if we live His Word—if we walk uprightly. What a wonderful, awesome, loving God we serve. So, enjoy the *goodness* of God and never again attribute evil to our wonderful heavenly Father.

Chapter Two

God Is Our Sufficiency, Fear Not!

To be a student of the Bible, we must understand words according to their biblical usage. As we do this, we are adhering to the word of God where it tells us that the Word is of "no private interpretation" (2 Peter 1:20). How we have defined and utilized the word *fear* has caused endless debate and problems for the man or woman attempting to walk in alignment and harmony with God.

I have learned over the years that fear is the ultimate f-word. God did not design man to fear Him but to love Him. Not only does God want us to walk without fear, He also instructs us how to overcome fear in our lives.

In 2 Corinthians 3:4-5, God tells us He is our sufficiency in all things: "*And such trust have we through Christ to God-ward: not that we are sufficient of ourselves to think anything as of ourselves; but our sufficiency is of God.*"

God is our sufficiency. According to Bullinger's *Critical Lexicon and Concordance of the English and Greek New Testament*, sufficiency is defined as "fitness, ability, competency." The word "of" in Greek, *ek*, is a preposition, a word placed in front of a noun or pronoun to show connection with or to something. *Ek* is used to describe the origin or source from which something derives. "But our sufficiency is of God" literally means that our fitness, ability, and competency come from God. God is the source of real life, He is the origin of my ability, fitness, and competency. Isn't that amazing? As I trust in God and His Word, He makes me fit, gives me spiritual ability, and makes me competent. And guess what else this verse tells me? A man without God can never really be considered fit, competent, or have real spiritual ability that comes from God.

But he [Jesus Christ] answered and said, every plant, which my heavenly Father hath not planted, shall be rooted up. Let them alone: they be blind leaders of the blind. And if the blind lead the blind, both shall fall into the ditch. (Matthew 15:13-14)

Our source and origin of strength as a believer in God is God Himself. God makes us strong as we believe His Word. God makes us competent as we believe His Word. According to David in Psalm 119, God makes us wiser than even our sense-knowledge teachers and our enemies as we believe His Word.

Thou [God] through thy commandments [meaning His Word] *hast made me wiser than mine enemies: for they are ever with me. I have more understanding than all my teachers: for thy testimonies are my mediation. (Psalms 119: 98-99)*

We can clearly see from God's Word that He is our source of strength, fitness, and ability. If God is our sufficiency, then why do we ever need to have fear? We never have to fear. Fear is never right or okay. For us to properly understand fear, we must see it, view it, and understand it from God's perspective, not from man's perspective. So, let us go to the word of God and see what the fountainhead of all truth has to say on this subject of fear. We will consider four points or perspectives on the subject matter of fear:

1. God's perspective on fear
2. The origin of fear
3. The consequences of fear
4. How to dispel fear

God's Perspective on Fear

God works on man's behalf based on man's belief in God and man's love for God. Fear is *not* of God. One of the biggest mistakes in the translation of the Bible was to use the English word "fear" when describing man's relationship with God. The word fear, when dealing with the relationship between God and man, would be better translated as awe, reverence, respect, or love. We are to be in awe of God. We are to revere, love, and respect God. We do this by loving, respecting, and being in awe of God's written Word. In reality, it is difficult to really love anyone or anything we are afraid of. If I fear, am in fright, dismay, or in terror of God, I cannot really love Him.

What are some of the things that God says about fear as it relates to our relationship with Him?

For God hath not given us the spirit of fear; but of power, and of love, and of a sound mind. (2 Timothy 1:7)

God has not given us the spirit of fear. Therefore, fear must come from another source. There was no fear in man prior to the first sin of man in Genesis 3. After man sinned, he had fear due to his loss of fellowship with God. Now, I know what some of you are thinking. "Isn't it okay to have a little fear at times?" If this is true, we should be able to trace it in the word of God. Look at Revelations 21:7-8:

He that overcometh shall inherit all things; and I will be his God, and he shall be my son. But the fearful, and unbelieving, and the abominable, and murders, and whoremongers, and sorcerers, and idolaters, and all liars, shall have their part in the lake which burneth with fire and brimstone: which is the second death.

In this verse, the heavenly Father gives a nice detailed list of actions that He does not approve of. A little fear is not okay, no matter how small it may be. If a little fear is okay, then according to this list other things are okay as well, just as long as they appear in small quantities (the "little" category). If this is our logic, then that means a little unbelief must be okay from time to time. Being a little abominable is okay with God, just as long as you only do it twice a year. A little murder is okay, right? Hey, a little whoremongering can't be too bad. Tell your spouse that; tell them whoremongering keeps the fire in the relationship. A little sorcery is okay. A little idolatry is good, right? See how ridiculous and illogical it sounds when you try to make certain behaviors okay based on the quantity of the behavior? If unbelief, whoremongering, murder, etc. are wrong no matter the amount, then *fear* is also wrong, no matter the amount of it we think we have. We should not walk in fear but trust the living God who is our sufficiency in everything.

I sought the Lord, and he heard me, and delivered me from all my fears. (Psalms 34:4)

David seeks God, and God delivers him from fear. If fear was okay or a great thing to have, then why would God deliver a person from something that was okay to have? It is because God knows fear is never okay. We may be tempted to fear, but that is when we must grab our minds, think, and find the scripture in the word of God that will deliver us from that particular fear we are facing at that moment.

And Moses said unto the people, Fear ye not, stand still, and see the salvation of the Lord, which he will shew you today: for the Egyptians whom ye have seen today, ye shall see them again no more for ever. The Lord shall fight for you, and ye shall hold your peace. (Exodus 14:13-14)

The Egyptians, who had enslaved the children of Israel for hundreds of years, were pursuing them to destroy them. Let me set the picture for you of what was really going on. God had provided Moses instructions to have Israel camp between two mountains (Exodus 14:2). So, Israel encamps between them and just in front of them was the Red Sea. Then, in hot pursuit are Pharaoh and the Egyptian army. In other words, Israel is absolutely surrounded, with no real escape plan, at least not one their five senses could recognize. Can you imagine the terror of the moment? Can you imagine how Israel might be questioning the leadership of Moses, God's man? After all, Moses just got them entrapped in a life-or-death situation. Yet, does Moses say boldly to the people, "Be afraid … be very afraid." No, he did not say that. Moses didn't even tell them it was okay for them to have a little fear. No, the man of God declared the truth of God to the people, which was "fear ye not."

Not only did Moses tell them not to be afraid, he provided them with reasons not to be afraid. They were given three clear-cut reasons not to be afraid in this situation. If they did not fear, three things would happen: (1) They would literally see the salvation of the Lord, (2) They would never again see their captors, the Egyptians, and (3) the Lord would fight for them. What a powerful moment for the children of Israel. Well, guess what happened? God fought for them just like Moses told them He would. Pharaoh and his army pursued Israel. God, via the hand of Moses, parted the Red Sea, and guess what happened? God fought for Israel and they saw the salvation of God, just as Moses had declared. Pharaoh and his army pursued Israel and drowned in the Red Sea. See the great deliverance that God makes available to those of us who believe Him and His Word and refuse to fear? God is our sufficiency in every situation and circumstance of life, so fear not!

Origin of Fear

Where does fear come from? We have already clearly seen that it does not come from our heavenly Father (2 Timothy 1:7). Fear is the tool that the god of this world (2 Corinthians 4:4) uses to defeat people, especially the born-again believers. How does fear defeat us? Fear brings unbelief. It causes a man or woman to not believe the promises of God. You must be fully persuaded of God's Word, with no doubt or fear, for the promise of God to come to pass in your life. Fear is an enemy that must be overcome and defeated by any born-again believer who truly desires to walk in power and in fellowship with their heavenly Father.

Consequences of Fear

There are consequences for the man or woman who walks in fear or who tolerates fear in their lives. The biggest consequence is that you will be placed in a trap where you are unable to believe God and His Word.

The fear of man bringeth a snare: but whoso putteth his trust in the Lord shall be safe. (Proverbs 29:25)

Whenever we fear, it will lead us to be caught in a snare or trap. A snare/trap is used by a hunter. The adversary is the hunter, and if we allow fear to take up residence in our thinking, we become the prey of the adversary.

Casting all your care upon him; for he [God] careth for you. Be sober, be vigilant; because your adversary the devil, as a roaring lion, walketh about, seeking whom he may devour. (1 Peter 5:7-8)

Another dynamic and power-packed verse. Look at the great knowledge and wisdom that God provides us about the devil. God uses the analogy to compare the devil to a lion. When a lion hunts, it often tracks its prey for days at a time. It uses the days of tracking as a time of observation of its prey, looking to pick up on tendencies, habits, and weaknesses of its eventual meal. Then, when it is ready to attack, it will roar. It uses its roar to freeze its prey. The roar of the lion induces *fear*. The second or two of the prey being unable to move from the *fear* of the roar allows the lion an extra second or two to pounce on its prey. The devil, as a roaring lion, walketh about seeking whom it may devour. The devil uses *fear* to freeze us! He uses it to intimidate us from moving in our minds to grasp our only defense against him—*the word of God*. Yet, God is always crying out to us: "*Fear not, I am thy sufficiency!*"

Also notice in these verses that three key words come up that help us understand how *not* to become the meal of the adversary. Those three words are: *casting, sober,* and *vigilant*. A deeper understanding of these words helps us form a powerful defense against the roaring lion, the devil. Each one of these words builds off the other and forms a mathematical equation for us to implement in our lives. Any breakdown in the equation causes the entire thing to fall apart, causing us to be defenseless against the devil. The word *cast* is defined as "to hurl with sudden motion with a mindset to lay aside burdens." What are we to cast, and who are we to cast it to? We are to cast away all of our care. Here, care is defined as "anxiety." Anything that makes us feel anxious is to be hurled with a sudden motion to God.

Why are we to do this? What leads to our anxiety? Fear is a great divider of the mind. Fear and anxiety work in concert to divide the mind, causing the mind to begin to breakdown so that it cannot track with the word of God. Fear and anxiety are weapons used by the devil to cause one to literally forget what the word of God says. If I forget what the word of God says, more anxiety begins to build in my thinking. God, in His loving wisdom, gives us a caution flag. The warning is this: If I am anxious, then the temptation to fear is present. If fear is present, you can be sure that the roaring lion is lurking in the vicinity.

If I am full of anxiety, then I can't be sober. Sober is defined as "temperate, watchful, circumspect." Have you ever seen an intoxicated person? One who is intoxicated loses their balance; they can't walk straight or think straight. What is the opposite of intoxication? It is to be sober, balanced. The devil uses anxiety to lead us to lack balance in our lives. If we are out of balance in our thinking, our emotions, in life in general, we become an excellent candidate for the next meal of the adversary. Then, once I am out of balance in life, I can no longer be vigilant. Vigilant is defined as "to stay alert, be attentive, observant, watchful, to be awake when it is customary to sleep." Who should I be on the lookout for? Who should I be attentive of? Who should I be watchful for? The answer is the devil, the roaring lion who walks about seeking those he can devour, who he can steal from, who he can kill, and who he can destroy. (John 10:10)

Look at the weapons God gives us to fight against the devil. We cast all our anxiety to God so that we can remain sober, so that we can be vigilant against the roaring lion. If I don't cast away the anxiety, it eventually will get the best of me. It will keep me from remaining sober, cause me to become intoxicated mentally, and to lose my balance in life, which leads me to the place where I can't be vigilant against the one who is seeking to devour me. This entire process begins with us staying out of *fear*, learning to trust God with every single ounce of our lives. God's message is clear:

Fear not!

Casting leads to being sober,
Sober leads to being vigilant,
Vigilance leads to victory over the roaring lion, the devil.

So, how do I cast my care upon God? Simple, by remembering God's Word. When an attack or challenge comes in my life, I must get to the word of God in my thinking. As I focus on the Word, God can then remove the care and anxiety that I am experiencing. When the devil attacked Jesus Christ, he responded by telling the devil, "It is written." (Matthew 4:1-11/Luke 4:1-13) In other words, Jesus Christ exchanged the potential anxiety and fear of life for the word of God. We must do no less. We must exchange the fear, anxiety, and negativity of life for the word of God. As we keep the word of God the dominant focus of our thinking, we are less vulnerable to the fear and darkness that is promoted by the devil himself. Fear is always wrong, and like David we seek God via His Word to allow God to deliver us from all of our fears.

Here is another key for recognizing and overcoming fear. We must understand that there are *covers* for fear. Fear often rides in on other emotions. Situations, emotions, ideas, and other things can often be fronts for fear. Here are some covers for fear: ego, pride, anger, and sickness. Fear can hide behind ego. A person can use their ego to hide the real problem, which is their fear. Even sickness can be a cover for fear. Many times in life, I have dealt with people who have had long-term bouts with some kind of sickness or disease. You know how they got it? Fear. They feared having some disease, and that fear brought the disease right to their doorstep. Mother died of cancer, aunts died of cancer, so people begin to believe out of fear that they will die of cancer. This is what befell Job:

For the thing which I greatly feared is come upon me, and that which I was afraid of is come unto me. (Job 3:25)

The trials of Job (loss of property, death of children, sickness/disease, etc.) came upon him as a result of his fear. Here is another point of clarity regarding the devil and his nature. Have you ever heard the saying "give them an inch and they will take a mile"? This is exactly what the devil did to Job. Job had fear, but not enough to justify all the attacks he came under via the devil. Job gave the devil an inch due to his fear, and once in Job's life, the devil tried to wrack and ruin his life and bring total destruction. Yet with all that Job lost as a result of his fear, God was able to restore everything he lost and then some, due to Job getting the fear out of his life and taking a stand on the word of God (Job 42:10).

How to Avoid Fear

Now that we see that fear is wrong, we must begin the process of learning how to avoid it. The greatest key to overcoming and avoiding fear is to walk in the love of God.

There is no fear in love; but perfect [mature] *love casteth out fear: because fear hath torment. He that feareth is not made perfect in love. (1 John 4:18)*

Only our love for God can cast out fear. The local therapist can't cast out fear. Medication can't cast out fear. Only walking with the love of God burning in our hearts can rid us of fear. Fear and love can't occupy the same place; one or the other will dominate. No man can walk with a little fear and a little love at the same time. Love can, and will, cast fear out of a man's mind and life. Jesus Christ was fearless because he so loved God. You can walk in fearlessness as you walk in love. Notice in the verse that it says, "fear hath torment." In other words, fear will torment a man or woman if it is allowed to move, fester, and grow undetected. Ever had a rock in your shoe? One little rock in your shoe can drive you nuts. So, once you become aware of the rock in your shoe, what do you do? You sit down and take your shoe off so you can remove the rock. Then you put your shoe back on and begin walking again. You say to yourself, "Ah, it feels so much better since I got that stupid rock out of my shoe." We don't try to get comfortable with the rock in our shoe; we remove it. Neither should we try to get comfortable with fear. We remove fear in our lives by loving God and believing His Word!

So how do we avoid fear? We avoid fear by walking with great love in our hearts toward God. Not only must we love God, we must also know that God loves us.

For I am persuaded, that neither death, nor life, nor angels, nor principalities, nor powers, not things present, nor things to come, nor height, nor depth, nor any other creature, shall be able to separate us from the love of God, which is in Christ Jesus our Lord. (Romans 8:38-39)

"Let your conversation (conduct/behavior) be without covetousness; and be content with such things as ye have: for he (God) said, I will never leave thee, nor forsake thee. So that we may boldly say, The Lord is my helper, and I will not fear what man shall do unto me. (Hebrews 13:5-6)

Nothing can separate us from God's love, and God promises to never leave or forsake the born-again believer. We can walk with great love and power knowing that our heavenly Father is not against us but for us. We can walk with great confidence knowing that our heavenly Father will never leave or forsake us, also knowing that He is, and will always be, our sufficiency in every situation as we believe His written Word and promises to us.

We can avoid fear in our lives by trusting, relying on God's Word, by letting no one and no circumstance talk us out of what the heavenly Father has promised us. Trusting God is another great key to avoiding fear.

For I have heard the slander of many; fear was on every side; while they took counsel together against me, they devised to take away my life. But I trusted in thee, O Lord: I said, Thou art my God. My times are in thy hand: deliver me from the hand of mine enemies, and from them that persecute me. (Psalms 31:13-15)

Look at the confidence and boldness of David. He had confidence in God. "I have heard the slander of many," David said. The devil often uses our five senses against us. He attacks us via what we can see, hear, taste, touch, or feel. David "heard" the slander. The slander was really the devil's attempt to make David afraid. David was aware of those who took counsel against him, those who sought to take his life. The temptation to *fear* must have been monstrous for David. But by David's free-will choice, he chose to *trust* God over and above the sense-knowledge attack he was under. David opened his mouth and boldly declared of God, "Thou art my God. My times are in thy hand: deliver me from the hand of mine enemies and from them that persecute me." This is what a fearless man looks like, trusting His God above his challenge and circumstance in life. You also can walk with this kind of courage, boldness, and fearlessness as you put your trust in the God of your sufficiency.

Looking at the word of God, we have discovered and learned God's perspective on fear. We have seen where fear originates (the devil). We have seen the potential consequences of living with any quantity of fear, how fear is a snare and a trap. We have also seen, by way of the life of Job, the objective of the devil is to use fear to bring destruction to our lives. Yet, God in His wisdom has provided a way for us to walk out of fear by walking in the love of God and by trusting God with every ounce of our lives. We have learned the need to cast all our care and anxiety onto God so that we can walk with great spiritual sobriety, which allows us to gain the spiritual strength needed to remain vigilant against our ultimate enemy, the roaring lion, the devil. The call of God in our day and time is: God is our sufficiency, fear not!

Chapter Three

Keys to Overcoming Challenges

God's word is often so tender when describing us as "His children." Knowing that we are His children, God's nature is to be long-suffering with us as we grow, develop, and mature in our walk with Him. This principle has been evident in my own life for years. When I first became serious about a walk with God as my heavenly Father, I thought my decision to follow Him would lead me instantly to a life where I would have no more real challenges. I thought I would change addresses and move from "Sin Street" and go directly to a luxurious spiritual high-rise on "Comfort Street." Boy was I wrong, and what a shock to my system. As you read this and get honest, you will recognize that at one point, you may have believed like I did.

As I grew and matured, I came to quickly understand that becoming born again does not remove me from the *need* to be responsible for my life. What a revolution in my life, the day I discovered that God fights for me as I hold fast to His Word. So many Christian believers often get defeated in life and then blame God for their defeat. God helps me *win* and *overcome* in life as I trust and believe His Word. God makes promises to us, and He promises to perform His promise for us, but we have failed to recognize the missing element on our part.

And being fully persuaded that, what he [God] had promised, he was able also to perform. (Romans 4:21)

In this section of Scripture dealing with Abraham and his wife Sarah having a child way beyond the childbearing years, we see great keys in life for us to apply. Abraham was fully persuaded that what God had promised he was also able to perform (results are not always instantaneous). To the simple Bible reader, this verse appears to say that our heavenly Father does all the work, He promises and performs what He promises, and we do nothing but wait on our pay day. If we have these kinds of thoughts, it is no wonder why so many of us as Christians are defeated. What we have failed to see in this verse is the missing lynch pin between what God promises and what God performs. A lynch pin is used to connect things together. What connects the promise of God to the performance of God is our *believing* His promise. God promises, we choose to believe what He promises, and then God can and will perform what He promised. Remove the lynch pin of our believing and you tie God's hands from performing His promise in your life. God may desire to help you, but if we don't believe, if we are not fully persuaded of His Word like Abraham was in a challenging situation, we hinder the Father from working mightily in our lives. This is how the word of God works with great precision:

God promises via His Word

We believe His promise (His Word)
God performs what He promised.

Our believing or faith is the lynch pin that allows God's promise to connect to His performing of what He promised. Once I was able to grasp this, I was able to pray and believe God for so many things in my life. This principle led me to discover even greater depths of God's Word and allowed me to see the keys to overcoming challenges.

The thief [devil] *cometh not, but for to STEAL, and to KILL, and to DESTROY: I am come that they might have life and that they might have it more abundantly. (John 10:10)*

Here we see Jesus Christ getting to the crux of the matter regarding the devil. The devil shows up for one of three reasons: to steal, kill, or destroy. Those are his objectives. What is an objective? An objective is something that one works toward, a goal, a purpose. Our main challenge in life is to overcome the devil's objectives, to keep him from stealing, killing, and destroying in our lives and the lives of others.

The next question we need to ask ourselves is "What is a challenge?" The term challenge can be defined as "a call to engage in a contest of skill and strength, a call to fight." Keeping the adversary's objectives from coming to pass in your life will take tremendous skill and strength that can only be gained or ascertained from God's Word and the operation of Holy Spirit. Jesus Christ informed his disciples that the day would come when they would not only be able to do His work, but they would be capable of doing greater works than their Lord.

Verily, verily, I say unto you, He that believeth on me, the works that I do shall he do also; and greater works than these shall he do; because I go unto my Father. (John 14:12)

Jesus Christ overcame challenges. Therefore, as we do His works and even greater, we should overcome challenges as well.

These things I have spoken unto you, that in me ye might have peace. In the world ye shall have tribulation: but be of good cheer; I have overcome the world. (John 16:33)

As followers of the Lord Jesus Christ, we are to do what he did. In this verse, Jesus Christ states that he overcame the world. Therefore, we ought to be able to do the same. To overcome and be victorious in life, it will take us having the thought life of Jesus Christ and the concentrated, disciplined focus on God's Word as Jesus Christ had. Jesus Christ, of his own free will, saturated his mind and thoughts with the word of God. Once his mind was saturated with the word of God, he used his free-will choice to concentrate his mind on the Word he had saturated his mind and thoughts with. That is how he lived a victorious life, and we can do no better than our Lord.

For whatsoever is born of God overcometh the world: and this is the victory that overcometh the world, even our faith. Who is he that overcometh the world, but he that believeth that Jesus Christ is the Son of God? (1 John 5:4-5)

What a remarkable and powerful verse of scripture.

Whatsoever is born of God overcometh the world. How does one become born of God? God declares in His Word that to become born of Him is to confess Jesus as Lord and believe that God raised him from the dead (Romans 10:9-10). This process is called the new birth or being born again. The promise of 1 John is that anyone who is born of God overcometh as we believe or have faith in God and His Word. The verse also promises that we who believe that Jesus Christ is the Son of God overcometh. I can't believe whatever I want to believe and overcome challenges. To truly overcome in this life, I must be born of God via the new birth and believe that Jesus Christ is the Son of God. Then, and only then, can I have the assurance and confidence that I can overcome all challenges that I face in life. Notice the verse does not tell me to believe that Jesus Christ is a "nice guy" or that he is "just one of hundreds of religious teachers" or that he is "just a prophet." The word of God declares that he is the Son of God and that believing this is a core element in our ability to overcome.

Another key point in the scripture is that it declares that our victory in life is our faith—believing. How does one get faith? Are we simply born with it, or do we have to take some action to receive this faith? How important is faith? It is vitally important, for without it, one can't please God.

> *But without faith it is impossible to please him* [God]*: for he that cometh to God must believe that he is, and that he is a rewarder of them that diligently seek him. (Hebrews 11:6)*

Without faith (believing), the Word declares that it is

impossible for us to please God. Don't you want to please your heavenly Father? Of course, you do. Therefore, you need faith. So how do we get this vital element called faith? Every Eastern religion teaches that man is born with faith and a spark of the divine (spirit), and if man just places himself under some type of law or religious system, then his faith and spirit will be ignited by God. This is one of the great fallacies and deceptions used by the adversary in the world. Without the new birth, man has no spirit of God, and without believing the word of God, man has no access to faith.

So then faith cometh by hearing, and hearing by the Word of God. (Romans 10:17)

Faith comes by hearing the word of God—hearing it to the point that we believe it and take action on it. The word of God is the key. No word of God, no faith. Without belief in the word of God, one is unable to understand the new birth and how to receive it. No new birth, man remains a natural man dead in trespasses and sins. No word of God, no spiritual ability or spiritual enablement. No word of God, no access to the power of God that allows us to overcome every challenge we may face in life.

Now that we have laid a foundation for overcoming challenges in life, let us now go to three keys we can use on a daily basis to aid and lead us to overcoming obstacles and challenges in life. The three keys are:

1. The word of God
2. Being thankful

3. Knowing that God always makes a way to escape

The Word of God

When faced with a challenge, we must get to what the word of God says on the particular issue. When a challenge arises, we should ask ourselves "What does the word of God say?" To know what the word of God says, I must study it, learn it, and apply it in my daily life. The word of God must be the center of my life. I must conduct my life according to the word of God if I want the blessings of the Father. The word of God must be my compass, always directing me north, always directing my actions, speech, and life toward what will please my heavenly Father and what will ultimately defeat the adversary, the devil. The cultural norms of the day can't be my guide and compass. The politics of the day can't be my compass. Not even the religious traditions of the day can be my compass. My only compass has to be the word of God. Jesus Christ is the ultimate example of how the word of God is the key to success and victory in life.

Then was Jesus led up of the Spirit into the wilderness to be tempted of the devil. And when he had fasted forty days and forty nights, he was afterward an hungered. And when the tempter came to him, he said, If thou be the Son of God, command that these stones be made bread. But he answered and said, It is written, Man shall not live by bread alone, but by every word that proceedeth out of the mouth of God. (Matthew 4:1-4)

In this record, the devil himself comes and challenges Jesus Christ, tempts him. How did Jesus Christ respond?

He responded with the word of God and said to the devil, "It is written." Jesus Christ, the Son of God, fought the devil with the powerful word of God. What would ever make me think I could overcome the devil by any other means than that which Jesus Christ overcame him? The word of God is the key to overcoming challenges in life. Here's a question for you: How could Jesus Christ say, "It is written" if he had not studied and mastered the written word of God? He couldn't. Therefore, we clearly see that Jesus Christ knew the scriptures and that the scriptures were his defense against the attacks of the adversary. Notice, Jesus Christ did not quote the popular cultural trend of the day. He did not try to overcome the devil based on some political notion. He did not try to overcome the devil by quoting some famous entertainer or philosopher. Jesus Christ overcame the devil with the written word of God. He overcame by saying "It is written."

Jesus Christ made the word of God his compass, his habit, his practice. On the pages of the Scriptures are many examples of men and women who lived this word of God and received the corresponding blessing. Then there are examples of those who rejected the word of God and received the corresponding consequence. No other human being has ever mastered living the word of God to the degree that Jesus Christ did. The written word of God was the habit, the heartbeat of Jesus Christ, and we need to follow his example and make the Scriptures our habit and heartbeat.

I grew up playing sports. I played football, basketball, and ran track. In each sport, coaches emphasized the fundamentals of the sport. In football practice, we daily went over the same drills—over and over and over again until they became second nature. When I asked my coach why such a keen focus on the fundamentals, he revealed a lesson to me that I have never forgotten. He said to me, "I want these drills and techniques to become second nature to you. I want them to become your habit, because in the midst of competition and an athlete becomes tired or fatigued, his habits, good or bad, will come forth. In fact, your habits will make the difference between winning and losing."

I have never forgotten that lesson by a high school coach. Though I no longer play sports, the lesson I learned on that day has been applied to my walk with God and my competition against the ultimate opponent, the devil. If the word of God is my habit, then I don't have to worry what I will do when a challenge of life arises. I am going to do the word of God because I have made "It is written" my habit. The first key to overcoming any challenge in life is the written word of God.

Being Thankful

The second key to overcoming challenges is to be thankful. How can I be thankful in a challenging situation? I can be thankful because I know my heavenly Father loves me and will deliver His children from any kind of challenge or bondage. In fact, by way of His Son, Jesus Christ, he has already delivered us.

> *Wherefore he saith, when he* [Jesus Christ] *ascended up on high, he led captivity captive, and gave gifts unto men. (Ephesians 4:8)*

Anything that can captivate man, hold man in bondage, our God has already delivered us from by the life and ministry of His Son, Jesus Christ. Every sin, every sickness, every mental uncertainty, everything that could imprison us, Jesus Christ led it captive when he ascended back to the right hand of God. We are free in Christ Jesus. Therefore, I can be thankful in every challenge because I know it is God's will that I be free and remain free.

In everything give thanks: for this is the will of God in Christ Jesus concerning you. (1 Thessalonians 5:18)

In this verse, notice the detailed accuracy of the word of God. It says "in everything" give thanks. It does not say "for everything" give thanks. In vs. for is a huge distinction in this verse. If it said "for" everything give thanks, then I would have to give thanks to God for negatives, evil, and dark things that have been in my life or may come into my life. If I did that, I would be prescribing evil to my heavenly Father, which would be a sin, because the Word tells me that God is "light and in him is no darkness at all" (1 John 1:5). But I can give thanks "in everything" and not be prescribing evil to God.

For example, a crisis arises in my life that is financial in nature. I know that the crisis does not come from God, because His Word declares He wants me to prosper. The financial crisis comes from the adversary, yet I can be thankful in the situation for the deliverance and restoration of power of God over my finances. See the difference? I may become sick, but I know that sickness is not of God. However, I can be thankful for the word of God to claim over my sickness. I can say, "Father, I thank you for delivering me of this sickness based on your Word in 1 Peter 2:24 that says, 'by his stripes ye were healed.'" By doing this, I am thankful in the situation but not for the situation. By being thankful, I am also doing the will of God. In 1 Thessalonians, it says, "for this [giving of thanks in everything] is the will of God concerning you."

> *He* [God] *delivereth me from mine enemies: yea, thou liftest me up above those that rise up against me: thou hast delivered me from the violent man. Therefore will I give thanks unto thee, O Lord, among the heathen, and sing praises unto thy name. (Psalms 18:48-49)*

David declares that, due to the delivering power of God, he could give thanks. Staying thankful even in challenging situations allows the peace of God to rule in our hearts (Colossians 3:15). If God could deliver David, who was not even born again of God's Spirit, what can't our heavenly Father deliver us from who have received the new birth? He can deliver us from everything. Therefore, I can remain thankful because of the delivering power of God. Being thankful also aids us in having patience while we wait for the deliverance of God.

> *Cast not away therefore your confidence, which hath great recompense of reward. For ye have need of patience that after ye have done the will of God, ye might receive the promise. (Hebrews 10:35-36)*

Isn't God's Word absolutely amazing? Look at the

detailed wisdom and power of God in this verse. An unthankful man will never have confidence. Being thankful helps us remain confident in God's love and His ability to deliver us and bring to pass His promises in our lives. Becoming unthankful will cause us to quickly cast away our confidence in our heavenly Father. God says we have "need of patience." Being unthankful leads us to becoming impatient. Whenever we are thankful, we have great confidence and patience (endurance) in God and His ability to deliver us in challenging times. What did Paul and Silas do when they were imprisoned in the Book of Acts? They sang praises unto God (Acts 16:25). You think in the midst of their praise there might have been some words of thanks? Thankfulness to God always allows us to find the path that will ultimately bring our deliverance in challenging times and situations.

The word of God declares there will be times when we don't know what to pray for. Our not knowing what to pray for based on our senses God calls an infirmity.

> *Likewise the Spirit [God] also helpeth our infirmities* [it's infirmity, singular, in the Greek text]*: for we know not what we should pray for as we ought: but the Spirit* [Holy Spirit, gift in manifestation] *itself maketh intercession for us with groanings which cannot be uttered. (Romans 8:26)*

The gift of Holy Spirit makes intercession for us, and this is done by the manifestation of speaking in tongues. God gives the believer many reasons for speaking in tongues. One of them is that by speaking in tongues in our private prayer life, we not only give thanks to God, but the Word declares we give "thanks well."

For thou verily give thanks well, but the other is not edified. (1 Corinthians 14:17)

The context of this section of the Word in Corinthians is Paul noting the difference between praying with the spirit and praying with understanding. Praying with my understanding is to pray in the language I know (English), yet we can also pray in the spirit, which is to pray via speaking in tongues (supernaturally). Whenever I pray via speaking in tongues, the word of God declares I am giving thanks well. So, whenever I am in a challenging situation, I speak in tongues more, giving thanks well to the Father for delivering me from the particular challenge I am facing.

Knowing that God Always Makes a Way to Escape

The third key to overcoming challenges is to know that God always makes a way for us to escape in difficult and challenging times, as shown below in 1 Corinthians 10:13.

There hath no temptation taken you but such as is common to man: but God is faithful, who will not suffer [allow] *you to be tempted above that ye are able; but will with the temptation also make a way to escape, that ye may be able to bear it."*

In every challenge, in every situation where we might be tempted, God makes a way for us to escape. We must become convinced of this, and the only way to do so is to keep working the greatness of God's Word into our hearts and minds. God wants us to escape every situation that could lead to us being in bondage or harmed. If you are a parent, do you want your children hurt, harmed, or in bondage? Of course not, and neither does God want it for you and me.

A great key for understanding God's will that you escape is to know that God's escape plan will never contradict His Word. For example, let's look at finances again. You have made some poor decisions in handling your money. You are now deep in debt and don't know how to get out. God's escape plan will *not* be for you to sell drugs or play the lottery to change your financial situation. Both choices, selling drugs and gambling, are contradictions of God's Word. You can't gamble, win, and then say, "God works in mysterious ways." God does not work in mysterious ways. God works and operates according to His Word.

Another example: let us say you are having marital problems. Getting divorced is not God's escape plan. God tells us, by way of the ministry of His Son, Jesus Christ, that under the law of Moses, He allowed divorce only because of the hard hearts of the people (Matthew 19:5-8). When people stop living and doing the word of God, we become hard-hearted toward God and His Word, and then we become hard-hearted toward our spouse. The next thing you know, we are in divorce court dividing up property and children. God's escape plan is His Word. His Word can and will deliver you from any challenging situation in life.

Another great point in this area is to recognize that God's escape plan is *not* always something with bells and whistles. A great example of this is the record of Naaman in 2 Kings 5:1-14. Naaman was a great military leader and was described as being a "mighty man of valor," yet he had to deal with the challenge of being a leper. Obviously, Naaman desired deliverance from his leprosy. Through a maid, Naaman learned there was a prophet named Elisha in Samaria who the maid thought could heal Naaman. So, Naaman took his horses and chariot and came to Samaria where the prophet Elisha was. When Naaman and his entourage got to Elisha's house, Naaman was expecting bells and whistles in order to get delivered from his leprosy. What he got was so simple that Naaman's emotions got out of control and he became angry, to the point that God described him as being in a rage (2 Kings 5:12).

Why was Naaman in a rage? His expectations did not line up with God's. Naaman arrived at the house of Elisha, and his first expectation was that the prophet would come outside to meet him, but that did not happen. Elisha sent a messenger to provide Naaman instructions on how to get delivered. Can you imagine Naaman's mindset? "Who does the prophet think he is? Doesn't he know how far I had to travel to get here? He can't come out and meet me himself? And on top of that, he tells me to go wash myself in the dirty river. Shouldn't Elisha come out himself, call on God, and give me a magic show so I can get delivered?" (2 Kings 5:11).

From this record and the response of Naaman, we see that many times our so-called expectations are nothing more than self-centered religious egotism. Naaman said, "I thought. . ." (2 Kings 5:11). It is not about what we think. It is about what God thinks and whether we are willing to line up our thinking and expectations with what God says. Well, thank God that Naaman's servants were courageous and bold enough to speak up and help him see the greater truth, which was his deliverance.

And his servants came near, and spake unto him, and said, My father, if the prophet had bid thee do some great thing, wouldest thou not have done it? How much rather then, when he saith to thee, wash, and be clean? (2 Kings 5:13)

Naaman responded to the words of his servants, went and dipped himself seven times in the River Jordan, as the prophet had originally commanded, and received his deliverance. The great lesson here is not to allow our own sense-knowledge expectations to cause us to miss out on our deliverance. Our mindset should be to know that God makes a way for us to escape out of every challenge, and the deliverance does not always come in the form of the spectacular!

Another great and wonderful example of God making a way to escape is a record in 1 Samuel 21, when David flees from Saul. Fleeing for his life, David comes to the city of Gath, where King Achish is the ruler. The servants of King Achish recognize David and how David was more powerful than Saul among the people (1 Samuel 21:11).

And David laid up these words [of the servants] *in his heart, and was sore afraid* [Godly cautious] *of Achish the king of Gath (1 Samuel 21:12)*

David was not afraid. Using the word afraid is a poor King James' translation. David was cautious of the king. He knew that King Achish might feel the need to try to take his life, just as King Saul was attempting to. So, David literally moved with "Godly caution." The next thing that happened literally blew my mind, seeing how God provided a way for David to escape this situation.

> *And he* [David] *changed his behavior before them, and feigned himself mad in their hands, and scrabbled on the doors of the gate, and let his spittle fall down upon his beard. (1 Samuel 21:13)*

David literally acted as if he was insane. He scratched on the door of the gate and allowed spit to flow out of his mouth and down onto his beard. If you can vividly picture this event, it's hilarious. To escape this situation, David acted like he had just escaped from a mental institution. The greater question here is who told David to do this? God had been with David at every point and juncture of his flight from Saul, and God was with David now. That's right—it was God Almighty who guided David to feign being mentally insane to get out of the situation. The king became upset and questioned his servants as to why they would bring a "mad man" to him (1 Samuel 21:14-15). David was released from the custody of the king and, according to 1 Samuel 22:1, escaped to the cave Adullam.

How many of us would have done what David did, pretended to be insane in order to escape? Well, David did, and he got out of a dangerous situation. God will always make a way for us to escape, and sometimes God's escape route will be much different than we might expect. God's way to escape will always bring glory to Him and bring abundance and peace to the given situation.

God has shown us from His word that it is His will that

we overcome challenges. We have learned the three objectives of the adversary (steal, kill, and destroy), and that our challenge in life is to overcome these three objectives, no matter what form they take. We also learned that God provides us with three keys to overcome every challenge: we go to God's Word, we remain thankful, and we know and believe that God makes a way to escape. What a great, wonderful heavenly Father we have, one who desires that we overcome every challenge in life and has left us the ultimate example on how to overcome via his Son, our Lord Jesus Christ.

Chapter Four

The Character of God

We live in a big and diverse world, a world made up of many cultures. On a daily basis, we have the opportunity and privilege to interact with all kinds of people. Through these interactions, we begin to develop relationships. These relationships can become in-depth or remain shallow, based on our ability to get others to trust us and to gain their trust. Many times, gaining trust is directly connected to one's character. The more character one reveals, the better opportunity for me to determine if an in-depth relationship can develop or if it must remain shallow and fickle.

How does one define character? According to the *New Random House Dictionary*, character is defined as "qualities making up an individual and/or the nature of a thing." Thinking about this definition sparked my mind and led me to contemplate if God has a character, and if so, what are the qualities that make up God's character and nature. As I began working the word of God, I discovered that not only does God have character, but his character is vast and dynamic.

So, with this teaching, we want to look at several things: (1) what makes up God's character, (2) how Jesus Christ manifested and revealed the character of his God and Father, and (3) how we as born-again believers are to show the character of God to the world.

So, what qualities actually make up the character or nature of God? Let me say from the outset, if I had all the time in the world and the oceans were my ink, I could never write enough about the character of God. So, what you will read here will simply be a few of God's qualities that make Him who He is. I think this work will be a beginning for further study on the character of God, not a final work. Through my study of the character of God, I discovered that He is:

1. A God of truth (Deuteronomy 32:4, Numbers 23:19, Titus 1:1-2)
2. A God of grace (1 Peter 5:10)
3. A God of peace (Romans 15:33, Isaiah 26:3, Isaiah 32:17, Psalms 85:10)
4. A God of patience (Romans 15:5)
5. A God of comfort (Romans 15:5, 2 Corinthians 1:3)
6. A God of hope (Romans 15:13)
7. A God of love (2 Corinthians 13:11)
8. A God of glory (Acts 7:1-2)

Let me say here that in my study I never saw God describe himself as a God of death or destruction. In my previous chapter, "The Goodness of God," I show you directly from the word of God that He is not the author of death and destruction. Death and destruction are not a part of God's character or nature, but they are a part of the devil's. So, let us begin looking a little deeper at the character of God by reviewing and studying what God says of Himself in His Word. In this study/teaching, I will not cover all eight of the above characteristics, but will look at a few. The remaining characteristics open a door for greater study and possibilities, as I have provided you with some Scriptures to look at while you study the other characteristics of God.

God of Truth

Because I will publish the name of the Lord: ascribe ye greatness unto our God. He is the Rock, his work is perfect: for all his ways are judgment [justice]*: a God of truth and without iniquity, just and right is he* [God]. *(Deuteronomy 32:3-4)*

In this verse, Moses is speaking to Israel. Moses lays out for the children of Israel the right view and perspective they are to have towards God. He informs them to only "ascribe greatness unto our God," never negatives like death, destruction, sickness, etc. Moses goes further into describing the character of God by saying that God's work is perfect. Then Moses culminates all of what he is saying by telling Israel *and us* that God is a "God of truth." Since God is a God of truth, then *all* truth must originate with Him. Therefore, if one is truly searching for truth, one must begin that search by looking into God and His word. My search for truth can't begin with science, history, mathematics, etc. My search must *always* begin with the God of truth. Science, history, and many other disciplines can reveal aspects of truth, but as one who has received the new birth, I must always remember that all truth originates with God. Since God is the God of truth, then the words that come from God must also be truth, and Jesus Christ taught this to us in his prayer to God in

John 17:17: "*Sanctify them through thy truth: thy word is truth.*"

You can never separate God from his Word. God's Word is as much God as God is God. Hence, when the God of truth decides to speak on a subject matter, then what He speaks will be truth.

> *God is not a man that he should lie; neither the son of man, that he should repent: hath he* [God] *said, and shall he not do it? Or hath he spoken, and shall he not make it good? (Numbers 23:19)*

If God has spoken it, He will bring it to pass. This verse is a tremendous lever for our prayer life. When we pray, we are praying to the God of truth. We are praying to a God who promises to back up His Word. We are praying to a God who can't lie. What great assurance we have when we pray to the God of truth.

> *Paul, a servant of God, and an apostle of Jesus Christ, according to the faith of God's elect, and the acknowledging of the truth which is after godliness; in hope of eternal life, which God, that cannot lie, promised before the world began. (Titus 1:1-2)*

What a breathtaking truth. The God of truth cannot lie. It is not that God simply chooses not to lie—it is that He cannot lie, for lying is not a part of His character or nature. God cannot embellish, He cannot stretch the truth, and He does not lie. It's not a part of His character. Why? Because He is the God of truth!

God of Grace

Our God is a God of grace. What is grace? Grace can be defined as God's divine, unmerited favor. Unmerited means you did nothing to deserve it, earn it, or warrant it. All favor comes from the God of grace. Simple, good, and wonderful things that come into our lives on a daily basis come from the God of grace.

One day I was standing in line for lunch, thinking about all the things I had to do when I got back to work from my break. There was a man in front of me who just seemed like he was having a great day as he engaged the cashier in conversation. This man took one glance over his shoulder at me, smiled, and turned back to the cashier and said to her, "I'm paying for his lunch also."

I looked at this man and graciously smiled and said, "That is very nice of you, sir, but you don't have to do that."

He replied, "I want to, so let me." This man, who I had never seen prior to that moment, bought my lunch that day.

As I walked away with my lunch, I softly said, "Thank you, Father." I did nothing to deserve, earn, or warrant a total stranger buying me lunch that day. This is an example of the God of grace working in my life. The man who bought my lunch had no idea that a born-again son of God was standing behind him in the lunch line that day, but God knew. God, who wants to favor His people, worked in that man's heart on that particular day to bless my life and show me favor. The God of grace wants to share His grace with His children. He wants to share His favor with His people. I am often reminded of the comments of that stranger that day: "I want to, so let me." God says the same thing to us: "I want to show you my favor, so let me."

But the God of all grace, who hath called us unto his eternal glory by Christ Jesus, after that ye have suffered awhile, make you perfect, stablish, strengthen, settle you. (1 Peter 5:10)

God is the God of "all grace." Not just a little grace, but all grace. This is why I said earlier that all grace, unmerited favor, comes from God. God is the origin of grace, but He can work in a person's heart—the person becomes the agent of God's grace—to move on your behalf to manifest God's favor in your life. Our very salvation is by God's grace.

For by grace are ye saved through faith; and that not of yourselves: it is the gift of God: not of works, lest any man should boast. (Ephesians 2:8-9)

I am not saved by my own works or doings, but I am saved by the accomplished works of God's Son, Jesus Christ. If I could save myself, then I could boast, says the Scriptures, but my salvation was not accomplished by any good work I did. It was by God's divine unmerited favor (His grace), which is wrapped up and encapsulated in what God did for us through His Son, Jesus Christ. Our God is the God of all grace!

God of Peace

Peace is a tremendous part of our heavenly Father's character and nature. He is the God of peace, as shown in Romans 15:33: "*Now the God of peace be with you all. Amen.*"

In Bullinger's *Critical Greek Lexicon to the New Testament,* the word 'peace' is defined as "undisturbed believing." God can grant such peace that man can live day by day without great disturbance to his believing or faith. The devil is always trying to steal or hinder our ability to have peace, but our heavenly Father is the true source and origin of real peace. Our ability to have peace is contingent upon our thinking, confession, and actions being in harmony with God's word and will. No one can believe whatever they want to believe and have real peace that comes from God. For me to have peace, it takes some work on my part to ascertain God's peace. God's peace is *not* automatic. Peace is now available to us through the accomplished works of Jesus Christ, and I bring this peace into manifestation based on how faithfully I keep my thinking, confession, and actions lined up with God's Word in light of what God wrought or accomplished for us through His Son, Jesus Christ.

Thou wilt keep him in perfect peace, whose mind is stayed on thee: because he trusteth in thee. (Isaiah 26:3)

In this verse, God promises to provide us with perfect peace if we meet the condition for the peace. The perfect peace can only come as we keep our minds stayed on God. How does one keep their mind stayed on God, since God is Spirit? (John 4:24). God reveals himself through His Word. As I keep my mind on God's Word, I am keeping my mind on God, for God is one with His Word. As I meet the condition, keeping my mind on Him, then God does His part and brings perfect peace to my life. In Isaiah 26:3, there are two responsible parties in this verse, the believer and God. I am responsible for keeping my mind stayed on God, and God is responsible for bringing me perfect peace. I can never do God's part (provide myself perfect peace), and God can never do my part (force or make my mind stay on Him). As I labor with God—me doing my part and He doing His—peace is obtained.

And the work of righteousness shall be peace; and the effect of righteousness quietness and assurance forever. (Isaiah 32: 17)

In the Old Testament, for a believer in God to be considered righteous, they had to live in harmony with the law and commandments of God. If the Old Testament believer ever violated God's law, he or she would become unrighteous in the eyes of God. Therefore, sacrifices had to be made for sin, and this work was done by the priests of Israel. In the New Testament, the believer is made righteous by God through the accomplished works of Jesus Christ, who was God's perfect sacrifice for sin and the ultimate high priest (Hebrews 7:24-27). As the Old Testament believer did the work of righteousness, he or she had peace. In the Old Testament, righteousness could be summed up as right thinking and living according to God's Word. As they thought right and lived right according to God's Word, they obtained peace, quietness, and assurance forever. We, in the New Testament, must do the same; we must think, confess, and act according to the word of God under the new covenant.

The significant difference between the old covenant and new covenant is that under the old covenant one could lose their righteousness, but under the new covenant, a believer can never lose their righteousness. However, if we don't line up our thinking, confession, and actions with God's Word, we can never experience or bring into manifestation the peace of God. Hence, this verse in Isaiah continues to illuminate for the believer in the New Testament how to bring the peace that God promises into practical reality.

Mercy and truth are met together; righteousness and peace have kissed each other. (Psalms 85:10)

Once again, the accuracy of God's Word is breathtaking and amazing. The verse declares that mercy and truth have met together, but righteousness and peace have kissed each other. Kiss is a much more intimate term than the word *met*. God is communicating to us here that there is a divine, intimate connection between righteousness and peace. They are as affectionate toward each other as a kiss between a man and woman. Also notice the order of the words in this verse. Righteousness proceeds peace. As I think in harmony with God's Word, as I speak/confess in harmony with God's Word, and as I take action that is in harmony with God's Word, the peace that God has for me will become evident. Our God of peace desires to truly share His peace with us; we just have to follow and obey what His Word informs us to do.

Therefore being justified by faith we have peace with God through our Lord Jesus Christ. (Romans 5:1)

We have peace with God. God does not hate us. God is not turning His back on us. We have peace with God. The word *have* is in the past tense, meaning it is done, it is completed, nothing left to do to get this peace but line up our thinking, confession, and actions with God's Word. No more keeping of the law to earn God's peace. We now live according to a higher law, the law of love, loving God and loving my neighbor (Matthew 22:36-40). The God of peace has come and done a perfect redeeming work through His Son, Jesus Christ. This perfect redeeming work is what grants us total access to God and His peace, joy, grace, and mercy. What a God of peace we have (Ephesians 2:19).

Now let's take a look at the role of Jesus Christ in manifesting the character of God to the world and our ability as born-again believers to do the same. In the gospel of John, it is declared that Jesus Christ came to declare God (John 1:19). The word 'declared' here means to "make known or reveal." So, we see that part of Jesus Christ's mission and ministry was to make known and reveal God to the people. In light of doing this, Jesus Christ would have made known or manifested the various characteristics of God on a horizontal level, so that man could see what God was like.

> *Then answered Jesus and said unto them, Verily, verily, I say unto you, The Son can do nothing of himself, but what he seeth the Father do: for what things soever he doeth, these also doeth the Son likewise. (John 5:19)*

Jesus Christ declares he could do nothing of himself, but he could follow the example of God and copy whatever he saw the Father do. Jesus Christ learned by observing his Father in action. How could he observe the Father in action? There would have been two ways for him to do that:

(1) study of the word of God, and (2) the operation and manifestation of holy spirit. Jesus Christ would have mastered the written word of God in the Old Testament. Through his mastery of the Scriptures, he would have seen God in action via the written word of God. Next, Jesus Christ operated holy spirit, whereby he would have received from God word of knowledge, word of wisdom, and discerning of spirits. Then by the manifestation of believing, miracles, and gifts of healing, Jesus Christ would have carried out the will of his Father. Through the written word of God and the manifestation of holy spirit, Jesus Christ would have seen the character of God on an intimate basis. So, as Jesus Christ declared God's Word and carried out his Father's will, what do you think he was showing mankind on a horizontal basis? He would have been showing us that God is a God of truth, grace, peace, patience, comfort, etc. As Jesus Christ declared God and showed us God's character, Jesus Christ himself would have been transformed by the character of God. In other words, Jesus Christ would have to be a man of truth, grace, peace, patience, comfort, etc. Jesus Christ shows us the character of God by literally manifesting the character of God on the level of the senses, so that the senses-dominated man could see God. What an amazing revelation to our souls if we only understood this.

Verily, verily, I say unto you, He that believeth on me, the works that I do shall he do also; and greater works than these shall he do; because I go unto the Father. (John 14:12)

Jesus Christ plainly and clearly declares that anyone who

believes in him can do the works he did and even greater works than he did. We have already shown that part of the work of Jesus Christ was to make known the Father by manifesting the character of God on a horizontal level. We as born-again believers are to make known the Father and show the world the Father living in us as we manifest the Father's character, just like Jesus Christ did. We accept the new birth (Romans 10:9. 10) and then we renew our minds (Romans 12:1-2) to the greatness of God's Word, which then transforms us and allows God's character to become our character. We become men and women of truth, grace, peace, patience, power, love, etc. We then do the works of Jesus Christ, standing in his stead, as Paul declared to us in the word of God.

Now then we are ambassadors for Christ, as though God did beseech you by us: we pray you in Christ's stead, be ye reconciled to God. (2 Corinthians 5:20)

God was in Christ reconciling the world unto himself, according to 2 Corinthians 5:19. Jesus Christ is no longer physically on the earth. Hence, the born-again believer now has the awesome privilege and responsibility of standing in Christ's place and reconciling the world (the people) back to God, one person at a time. We now represent God and His Son, Jesus Christ. What an awesome privilege we have. How can we reconcile man back to God? The world does not know God, and the only way it can know Him is for a real, live, flesh-and-blood human being to stand on this earth and once again declare, make known, God by revealing God's character via the preached and taught word of

God. Who would not want to be reconciled to a God of truth, grace, and peace?

Be ye therefore followers of God, as dear children. (Ephesians 5:1)

The word *follower* in the Greek literally means to "copy or mimic." We are to so develop ourselves in this word of God that we literally become copies or mimics of our heavenly Father. We should desire to copy His character. We should want to be men and women of truth, grace, love, and glory just like our heavenly Father. We should have the loving, tender heart of a child and say to the world, "When I grow up, I want to be just like my daddy." Yes, God is our Father now that we have received the new birth (Romans 10:9, 10), and He allows us to manifest His character to the world. He allows us to come to know Him on the most intimate terms. He allows us to have a wonderful relationship with him based on His Word and who He is. I hope you look forward to even a deeper walk with your heavenly Father as you begin to see and understand on a much deeper level the true nature and character of God.

Chapter Five

Freedom in Christ

I know most people enjoy a great movie from time to time. If I asked you what your top ten favorite movies of all time were, you could tell me very easily. I'm sure your list would be varied and include dramas, action, documentaries, etc. One of my favorite movies was done by Mel Gibson, *Braveheart*. As I watched the movie, especially the battle/war scenes, I often imagined that what I was seeing was similar to the battles that the children of Israel faced in the Old Testament. The intrigue of Scotland trying to throw off the shackles of English domination sparked my interest. Seeing how William Wallace, the character played by Mel Gibson, rose to a leadership position reminded me of men of the Scripture and how they developed leadership qualities and rose to higher positions. Men of God in the Bible often arise at a time where there is political upheaval or a time of oppression. Moses arose during the enslavement of Israel in Egypt. Daniel arose during the time of the Babylonian captivity of Israel. Even Jesus Christ came to birth at a time of a great political crossroad.

During *Braveheart*, the theme of freedom was constantly reinforced. Some of the most intense and electrifying scenes in the movie were when William Wallace was discussing the vitality of the people of Scotland having freedom. Remember the great lines of the movie? "What will you do without freedom?" "They may take our lives, but they will never take our freedom." Then the movie comes to the great climax, where William Wallace is finally captured. He knows that he is about to face death at his execution the next day. He turns to God and asks for strength to face what he is about to endure. The next day, the process of torture and execution begins. As the torture grows more brutal, William Wallace is told to just cry out for mercy and the execution will be swift. As Mel Gibson gasps for breath, you can see he is trying to muster the last ounce of strength he has to make one final statement. As the leader of the execution tells the crowd the prisoner has something to say, you can hear a hush go over the crowd, as they want to hear the man who fought them cry out for mercy. With his last breath, William Wallace cries out "FREEEEEDOOOOM."

The cry of and for freedom is God's call to the believer and to humanity! God wants people to be free from any kind of bondage. There is a spiritual battle that is raging just below the senses realm. Natural man can't see this war with the naked eye. This great battle is for the enslavement or freedom of humanity. The devil wants to enslave humanity, while our loving heavenly Father wants to provide man his true freedom. God is, and always has been, committed to freedom.

Wherefore he saith, When he ascended up on high, he led captivity captive and gave gifts unto men. (Ephesians 4:8)

The above verse shows and demonstrates that God is one hundred percent committed to freedom. The verse also shows us one of the great works that Jesus Christ accomplished for us—our true and ultimate liberation. During the ascension of Jesus Christ, he took *everything* that would ever enslave a man or woman and led that captivity captive. We are now free in Christ Jesus. It's the devil who does not want this knowledge made known or published in any shape or form, but we have been made totally free in Christ Jesus. God wants you free. With freedom comes mistakes, but God is so committed to freedom that He would rather have you and I free under Him, making mistakes, than to ever have us enslaved or in bondage to anything else. What a remarkable and dynamic truth to sink our teeth and lives into. God does not want us to be halfway free; he wants us totally free. God wants us free from sickness, disease, fear, worry, our past, etc.

Why freedom, God? God knows that without true, genuine freedom, it is impossible for you to develop and enjoy a relationship with Him. Therefore, God moves to free us so that we can enjoy our fellowship with Him. Such things like sickness and fear hinder our relationship with our heavenly Father. Therefore, God removes all barriers and impediments to our fellowship with Him. In my daily employment, I have had to visit young people in detention centers. I have seen them visit family members while there. In jail, the accused offender is typically placed on one side of a glass, while their love ones are on the opposite. To talk with each other, they have to use a phone that is placed on either side of the glass. Can they see each other? Yes. Can they talk to each other? Yes. Can they tell stories to each other? Yes. Can they touch each other? No. There is a barrier between them that ultimately hinders their relationship, their fellowship. The same goes for us with our heavenly Father; He wants no barrier between us and Him.

We must also distinguish the difference between the world's definition of freedom and God's. To the world, freedom means the right to be unloving, unkind, perverted, to disregard authority, etc. In other words, freedom to the world means anarchy on some level. Freedom to God means that he removes all bondage, enslavement, and barriers from us so that we can truly become our best for Him. Freedom to God is our right to fully engage in a relationship with Him without barriers.

For brethren, ye have been called unto liberty; only use not your liberty for an occasion to the flesh, but by love serve one another. (Galatians 5:13)

Using liberty for an occasion to the flesh is exactly what the world does. People say, "I'm free, therefore I can do anything I want. If I want to use drugs, I'm free to do that. If I want to be perverted, I'm an adult and I'm free to do that. If I want to rebel against any standard of truth, I am free to do that." From God's spiritual perspective, this mindset is one hundred percent incorrect. For the true believer, our freedom is for the expressed purpose of serving God and serving one another.

What is the opposite of freedom? I would say that it is bondage. Bondage will always be rooted in two things: a lie and fear. Whenever people are placed in bondage in some fashion, it is because they have accepted some lie or have tolerated fear in their lives. The devil moves lies and fear to ensnare and place humanity in bondage. The devil has used these tactics since the world began, and he continues to use them today. Why ever change your method of operation if what you are doing is so successful? We see these two tactics as far back as the garden of Eden. God placed Adam and Eve in the garden and gave them great freedom. However, He did provide them with some clear-cut instructions.

But of the tree of the knowledge of good and evil, thou shalt not eat of it: for in the day that thou eatest thereof thou shalt surely die. (Genesis 2:17)

Pretty clear instructions, right? But now let's move forward to Genesis chapter 3 and see how this all unfolds once the enemy of God, the father of lies, shows up in the garden of Eden.

And the serpent said unto the woman, Ye shall not surely die: For God doth know that in the day ye eat thereof, then your eyes shall be opened, and ye shall be as gods, knowing good and evil. (Genesis 3:4-5)

Through the record of Genesis 3, we see the devil unveil a crafty and deceitful plan. In verses 1-3, he gets Eve to add to the word of God *and* take away from the word of God. By doing this, the devil gets Eve to the spiritual position where He can finally unleash his two ultimate weapons on the rest of humanity. In verse 4, the devil tells a bold-face lie. He tells Eve that by eating of the fruit of the tree of knowledge, she would not "surely die." That is a lie. The bigger lesson learned here is that the devil lied to Eve, convincing her that she could disobey God and there would be no consequences. This continues to be *the* lie that he works over humanity with, persuading people that they can faithfully and habitually disobey God and there will be no consequences. This lie, along with many others, has brought people to the place of bondage.

Not only did the devil deceive Eve with this lie, he also was able to introduce fear into her mind in verse 5. There, the devil brought Eve to the place where she thought that God was hiding something from her. She began to consider that her wonderful, awesome God was lying to her and withholding things from her. This consideration led Eve to the ultimate f-word, *fear*. She feared that God was keeping things from her, and she accepted the lie that she could go against what God commanded and still have no consequences. In one grand record, you see how the devil uses fear and lies to captivate, ensnare, and bring bondage. If Adam and Eve had just obeyed God rather than falling prey to the adversary's wicked tools of fear and lying, humanity would not be in the place it is today. Another great truth we can glean from this record is that obedience to God is the ultimate freedom. The devil continues to persuade people that obeying God is bondage and real freedom is in doing whatever you want.

The Lord Jesus Christ brings us additional light on the subject of fear and lying, by crystallizing once and for all who is the author of lies in the book of John. Look at the thunderbolt of truth that Jesus Christ hurls at the religious leaders of his day in John 8:44.

Ye are of your father the devil, and the lust of your father ye will do. He [the devil] *was a murder from the beginning, and abode not in the truth, because there is no truth in him. When he speaketh a lie, he speaketh of his own: for he is a liar, and the father of it.*

What an amazing truth! The devil is a liar and the father (author, originator) of it. So, by moving fear and lies, the devil is able to rob humanity of the freedom that is theirs in Christ. Look at the great contrast at work here: the devil is a liar and the father of it, while Jesus Christ is the way, the truth, and the life (John 14:6). All of humanity now has to choose which route they will take. One route is carved out by the devil, based on fear and lies, that leads to death and destruction. The other route is carved out by the one sent from God, Jesus Christ, that leads us to a life that is founded on the truth of God's Word and brings us to a more than abundant life. (John 10:10).

The devil uses many avenues or fronts to get to us. One of those fronts is the individuals themselves. The devil seeks to work his way into our thinking and then hide there, day after day, week after week, and year after year. He will hide in the way we have been raised, he will hide in our culture, he will hide in our political beliefs, he will hide in our habits of life, and the list goes on. Therefore, our challenge as a true believer is to not allow the devil to hide in our thinking! We must continuously expose our minds to the light of God's Word. No one can control my thinking for me. Therefore, by free will, choice, I must always expose my mind to the light of God's Word to keep the enemy out of my nest, out of my thinking and actions.

And this is the condemnation, that light is come into the world, and men loved darkness rather than light, because their deeds were evil. For every one that doeth evil hateth the light, neither cometh to the light, lest his deeds should be reproved. But he that doeth truth cometh to the light, that his deeds may be made manifest, that they are wrought in God. (John 3:19-21)

If I love the truth and want to practice the truth, then I must keep coming to the light of the word of God to ensure that my deeds (actions) are in God. By continuing to expose my mind and life to the truth of God's Word and then living according to the Word I have exposed myself to, I allow myself to continue in the freedom that is in Christ Jesus. This process can be challenging at times, but very necessary. Many believers in God frequently want to talk or deal with those areas in life that they are good at. Few want to do the work on those areas where they are weak.

Let us examine this through a sports analogy. You have a young man who is a basketball player. He plays great defense and can shoot the ball "lights out." There is only one problem—he can't dribble the ball well. Therefore, he can only shoot if one of his teammates sets a pick for him. So, every day this player is in the gym working on his game, his skills. He works on his footwork for defense. He works on his jump shot by taking two hundred shots, both long-range and mid-range shots. However, he continues to avoid working on his dribbling. The season begins and he starts off red hot. He is consistently coming off picks and hitting his jump shot with ease. The season goes on and teams begin to see his weakness, his inability to dribble well enough to create his own shot. Therefore, teams adjust the way they play defense on him, and before you know it, he is not scoring as easily as he once did and is becoming frustrated. Why? He failed to address his specific area of weakness on the basketball court. Did he spend long hours in the gym? He most certainly did, but he did not address the specific area of weakness that would have made him a better basketball player.

So it is with walking with God. We need to address our specific area of weakness if we are going to improve and remain free in Christ Jesus in a practical manner. I have heard Christians instruct other Christians to simply read any part of the word of God on a daily basis. They justify this admonition by saying that reading any part of the word of God daily is better than not reading at all. I would say that is only partially true. The devil is not going to attack me where I am strong but where I am weak. I need to strengthen my weak areas, and that takes studying and applying specific verses and sections of the word of God.

For example, let us say my marriage is struggling. Will studying the Word on tithing help my struggling marriage? Highly unlikely. Therefore, I need to get to the specific areas of the word of God that will address my specific weakness or need. We don't want to be like the basketball player, spending all of our training time doing what we are already good at. We want to improve all areas of our game or skills as a believer. Staying strong in our fundamentals is vital, but we must push to improve and advance ourselves in all areas of life. By doing this, we can maintain our practical freedom in Christ Jesus.

Then said Jesus to those Jews which believed on him, If ye continue in my word, then are ye my disciples indeed; and ye shall know the truth, and the truth shall make you free. (John 8:31-32)

Jesus Christ declares that by knowing the truth we are made free. The key word in that verse is "know." In the Greek manuscript, the word is *ginosko*. In Bullinger's *Critical Lexicon and Concordance to the English and Greek New Testament*, ginosko is defined as "to perceive, observe, obtain a knowledge of or insight into … it also denotes a personal and true relation between the person knowing and the object known, i.e. to be influenced by one's knowledge of the object, to suffer (allow) one's self to be determined thereby."

To really know the truth means that I live according to it. It means that I take action on the truth I know. This knowing is not just a simple knowledge of facts. We know many people whose heads are full of biblical knowledge, but that does not mean they are living and acting on what they know. By me living and acting on the word of God (the word of God that I permit, suffer, or allow to have influence over me), I know I am made free by that truth that I live.

Here is a question that we must ask and be reminded of on a daily basis. Who or what makes us free? If we continue in the context of John 8:36, we find out who really makes us free: "*If the Son therefore shall make you free, ye shall be free indeed.*"

Only Jesus Christ can make me free! I am made free by God through the accomplished works of His Son, Jesus Christ. No form of government can make me free. No political party can make me free. No political document can make me free. I am only made free by the accomplished works of the Lord Jesus Christ. Not knowing this truth has led countless people to be enslaved by some form of government. A great political battle is now raging in the United States. Some citizens believe that certain forces within the country are trying to wipe out democracy and bring in some other form of government. People are all up in arms about this, but to those of us who have accepted the accomplished works of Jesus Christ, I say to you, "You are already free in Christ Jesus, and no form of government can take your freedom."

Stop eating the junk offered to you by politicians and so-called clergy around the issues of freedom. Stop and smell the Scriptures for a moment. What form of government did Israel live under in Egypt? It was not a democracy, yet God took care of his people. God instructed Moses to stretch out his hand toward heaven "that there may be darkness over the land of Egypt, even darkness which may be felt" (Exodus 10:21). The record in Exodus declares that there was darkness in the land of Egypt for three days, yet in the midst of that darkness, God took care of his people, for Exodus 10:23 says, " *but all of Israel had light in their dwellings.*"

What form of government did the prophet Daniel live under? It was not a democracy, yet God protected and delivered Daniel. Daniel worshipped the one true God, and this led him to a rather frightening proposition—becoming a human snack for some hungry lions. Daniel was put into a lion's den overnight, and the next morning the king arose with the belief that Daniel would be dead, eaten to pieces by the lions. In Daniel 6:21, the king came to the lion's den and mockingly said, "O Daniel, servant of the living God, is thy God, whom thou servest continually, able to deliver thee from the lions?" Daniel cries out from the lion's den, "My God hath sent his angel, and shut the lion's mouths, that they have not hurt me …" (Daniel 6:22).

What form of government did Jesus Christ live under? He did not live under a democracy, yet he blazed a clear path of truth and freedom through his political system of the day that would allow any man or woman in any generation or culture to be free if they wanted to be. Time and time again, through the word of God, you see God delivering His people regardless of the political climate or form of government his people lived under. Our God is for freedom!

Do you want to remain free as a believer? Then you must know and recognize that the picture you carry of yourself on a daily basis will determine if you remain free or forfeit your freedom. You must never give up your spiritual identity. You must never allow anything to talk you out of who you are in Christ. If you lose your spiritual identity, you will forfeit your freedom that has been won for you by Jesus Christ.

Last, but certainly not least, I must give you the reader some of the "highways to bondage," those things that can steal your freedom and place you back under the yoke of bondage. Think of it this way: whenever you travel a great distance on a highway, you map out your course. If you know in advance that there will be certain roads or highways that hinder you from your destination, you avoid them. The following is a list of "highways" you must avoid if you want to maintain your freedom in Christ. (Feel free in your private study to add to the list of highways to avoid if you like.)

1. The highway of condemnation (Romans 8:1)
2. The highway of conformity (Romans 12:1-2)
3. The highway of selfishness (Romans 15:1-2)
4. The highway of bitterness (Hebrews 6:15)
5. The highway of unthankfulness (Romans 1:21)
6. The highway of fear (Proverbs 29:25)

Let us close this study on freedom in Christ by looking at Galatians 5:1:

Stand fast therefore in the liberty wherewith Christ hath made us free, and be not entangled again with the yoke of bondage.

We are to stand fast (firm, with commitment and resolve) in the liberty wherewith Christ hath made us free. This liberty spoken of here in Galatians 5:1 is liberty that is strictly based on the obedience of the individual believer. As we obey the word of God, we have freedom. There is *never* any freedom in disobeying God. Disobedience will always lead to some type of bondage or enslavement. Adam and Eve were fooled into thinking that real freedom was in disobeying God—were they ever wrong. We are still dealing with the consequences of their fallacy of thinking. Do you want to be free? Then stand committed and resolved to obey God so that you can maintain the liberty that was purchased for you by the precious life, sacrifice, and ministry of our Lord and Savior Jesus Christ.

Chapter Six

Overcoming to Reach the Goal

Everyone thinks, but not everyone thinks deeply and seriously. As Christians, as believers in God and His Son, our Lord Jesus Christ, it is vital that we learn to think deeply regarding the things of God. We must begin to truly meditate on this word of God, we must look at it from different angles and viewpoints, and we must turn it over in our minds in order to grasp, understand, and fully comprehend the true riches of God's Word.

Have you ever given substantial thought about the dignity of your calling by God? Have you considered the reality that God has taken those of us who are born again from damnation to eternal life? Have you considered that God has called us out of darkness into light and has made us His very own children? You hold a special place in the heart of God. You have a dignified position with your heavenly Father. Then there are those of us who I like to say have a calling within a calling. There are some of us who are not only God's child, but after becoming God's child have been called to have an energized ministry (Ephesians 4:11-12), where we get to serve God in a greater capacity by helping to perfect His people in their practical walk. We get to help

God's people become involved in the work of the ministry and the edifying of the body of Christ. What a call, what a life we have to live!

We have been summoned and invited by God to a life that is uniquely unique. We have been given a purpose and direction in this life by Almighty God. There is no longer a question of our call by God, but the question now is, "Have I answered God's call, and am I fulfilling the call?" We must know that if God has called us, then the enemy of God, the devil, also is aware of our calling. To simplify this, let me make you aware of the truth that there are only two things in life that can hinder you from answering or fulfilling the call of God in your life: you and the devil. The devil, knowing of our calling, places us immediately in a unique spiritual competition. As we move daily to fulfill and answer our call, the devil moves to stop or hinder our calling. In other words, welcome to the ultimate competition of life.

Jesus Christ tells us how the devil hinders in God's Word in John 10:10: "*The thief cometh not, but for to steal, and to kill, and to destroy.*" In this verse, the devil is the thief. The devil hinders us by way of his ability to steal, kill, and destroy. He wants to steal our calling from us. He wants to kill us if he can. He wants to destroy or render useless our ability to respond to and fulfill God's call. We also play a major role in this ultimate spiritual competition. God gives us clear instructions on what we, as individuals, must do to properly respond and fulfill His call on our lives.

Wherefore seeing we also are compassed about with so great a cloud of witnesses, let us lay aside every weight, and THE SIN which doth so easily beset us, and let us run with patience the race that is set before us. (Hebrews 12:1)

God uses a dynamic analogy in this verse to explain to us the nature of the spiritual competition and how we are to respond or compete in this competition. God uses a figure of speech to compare life to a race. We want to race for God as fast and as far as we can. To do this, God says we must lay aside every weight and the sin that slows us down or besets us.

Now, I have participated in the world of track and field. It is a wonderful sport that is super challenging. In this sport, you usually have two types of runners, sprinters and distance. Regardless of your particular race, you want to enter the race with the least amount of potential weight possible. That is why you see runners wearing the lightest clothing available. You see runners wearing specially designed shoes that are as light as a feather. This is done so that, if I am a sprinter, I can run as fast as I can without any unnecessary weight to slow me down. If I am a distance runner, I want the same advantage as a sprinter. I want to run my mile or three miles with the least resistance possible. Can you imagine yourself as a sprinter entering the starting blocks of the one hundred meters and looking to your left at the competitor next to you and seeing he is wearing boots? Can you imagine yourself about to run a marathon, look at the competitors next to you, and see they are completely outfitted in professional hockey or football uniforms? Would not make much sense, would it? Absolutely not! How fast and far would they travel in boots or a uniform? Don't get me wrong, they could still travel or race, but what is the probability that they would *win*? Not likely, huh? If we study the history of the inception of the Olympic games, we discover that many of the runners often ran naked. That is right—they competed or ran with no clothes on in order to have nothing weighing them down.

Look at the beauty of truth that God is trying to convey to the Christian believer. The only real way to compete in this spiritual contest against the devil is to lay aside everything that might slow us down. God is telling us that if we have eyes to see and ears to hear, to lay aside our fears, doubt, and worry. Lay aside our past and fear over the future. All these things and more can impede us from answering and fulfilling God's call on our lives. Not only must we lay aside every weight, we must also lay aside *the sin*. Read the verse again. You will see that God does not say lay aside *a sin*, but to lay aside *the sin*. If it said *a sin*, that would be a generalized directive from the Father, but God says *the sin*, which is a specific area of weakness in your life as a believer. In other words, what is the sin for my life may not be the sin for you, and vice versa.

Our heavenly Father gets up close and personal in this verse. We are God's children, and as His children, we grow and mature at different rates of speed. In fact, there are levels or stages of growth for all of us. But an important key to our growth is overcoming *the sin* for us individually at a particular stage of growth. If I want to grow to the next level, I must overcome the particular sin or weakness at my current level in order to reach the next. So, begin asking yourself, what is holding me back? What is hindering me from getting to the next stage of spiritual growth? What is in my life that keeps me from reaching my goal?

The wonderful perspective of this growth process is the

reality that all men and women of God, both past and present, had to go through it. Apostle Paul had to lay aside his past and his sin in order to fulfill the call of God on his life, as seen in Philippians 3:13-14:

Brethren, I count not myself to have apprehended: but this one thing I do, forgetting those things which are behind, and reaching forth unto those things which are before, I press toward the mark for the prize of the high calling of God in Christ Jesus.

Paul boldly declares that he has not yet arrived at the place he should be, but he knows to eventually get there he will have to forget (lay aside) those things that are behind him. Now, Paul had tons of forgetting to do; he had tons of things to lay aside. Remember, before he was Paul, he was the man Saul of Tarsus. He was the man in the first century who had political clout as well as religious pedigree. He used his clout and pedigree to pursue Christians in order to persecute them and have them killed or imprisoned. Then Saul had an amazing encounter with Jesus Christ and was given a new calling, a purpose and mission in life. His name was changed and he began his mission. Paul had to lay aside his past mistakes and sin to answer God's call on his life. Now, here is some comfort for you. I imagine that the majority of you who are reading this book have not had Christians killed. So, if Paul could lay aside his weight and sin, so can we!

Once Paul laid things aside, he did something else. He began to reach forth—push forth—toward what God had set in front of him to do. Do you think Paul had other challenges along the way of pressing toward that? Of course he did, or did we forget our opponent who Jesus Christ told us comes to steal, kill, and destroy? So, what did Paul have to do to remain in the spiritual competition and win? He had to stay focused! He could not allow the god of distractions to capture his attention by way of the senses realm and pull him away from the goal and calling on his life. Remember our earlier example of track and field? I have seen sprinters lose their race in the last three to five meters. Just as the race is coming to an end, the lead runner removes his focus from his lane and into the lane of another competitor. Just losing focus for a split second has caused many sprinters to finish in second or third place, when in reality they should have won the race. *Focus* on the prize of the high calling of God in Christ Jesus is vital so that we do not get distracted by the senses realm, hence failing to answer and fulfill God's call and purpose for our lives.

Now let us take a look at the disciples of Jesus Christ and one in particular named Peter. We will see by examining Peter how one may get distracted from the call of God, how the devil can use our particular weakness or sin against us. In addition, we will see that our God is full of grace, mercy, and longsuffering, which allows all of us to get back on track if and when we have not done what He has called us to do.

Peter was one of the original twelve disciples that Jesus Christ chose. Peter was intimately involved in the best ministry mentoring program ever put together by God. Peter, along with the other disciples, had the awesome privilege of being prepared for the Christian ministry by Jesus Christ, the Son of God. They were given the privilege of walking and living with Jesus Christ. They were given access to be trained for the ministry by the man with the greatest teaching ministry in the entire world. They were allowed to ask him questions. They were allowed to be eyewitnesses to the signs, miracles, and wonders performed by Jesus Christ. They were also involved in the reproof and correction of Jesus Christ, which was not always nice.

One day, Peter took it upon himself to confront and correct the Lord Jesus Christ. It was not Jesus Christ who needed correcting, it was Peter—and, boy, did he get it when Jesus looked Peter in the eye and told him to "get thee behind me, Satan" (Matthew 16:22-23). Yet, Peter hung in there and was present on the day of Jesus Christ's ascension and was given his ministry assignment, recorded in the following sections of the word of God:

Go ye therefore, and teach ALL NATIONS … (Matthew 28:19)

And he said unto them, Go ye into ALL THE WORLD, and preach the gospel to EVERY creature. (Mark 16:15)

And said unto them, Thus it is written, and thus it behooved Christ to suffer, and to rise from the dead the third day: And that repentance and remission of sins should be preached in his name among ALL NATIONS, beginning at Jerusalem. And ye are witnesses of these things. (Luke 24:46-48)

But ye shall receive power, after that the Holy Ghost is come upon you: and ye shall be witnesses unto me both in Jerusalem, and in all Judea, and in Samaria, and unto the UTTERMOST PART OF THE EARTH. (Acts 1:8)

As we read these verses, we can see very clearly that God

wanted his Word to have a universal focus, not a short-sighted nationalistic focus. God wanted these disciples to take the gospel message to the whole inhabited earth, beginning first at Jerusalem and then expanding from there. Jesus Christ declared early in his ministry that he was only sent to the lost sheep of the house of Israel and not Gentile nations (Matthew 15:24). But a new vision, mission, and focus came at the end of Jesus Christ's earthly ministry. Now the vision was for this word of God to go over the entire world.

Peter was present to hear this, as well as witness the huge ministry shift and focus. Here is a question to consider: if the disciples were instructed to take the Word to all nations, did that include Gentile nations? From the reading of the word of God, it is clear that Gentile nations are now included in the equation. However, Peter initially disobeyed and failed to take the word of God to them. Peter continued to minister only among those who were of Israel, but God's call to Peter and the other disciples was to go worldwide. What happened? What did Peter fail to lay aside? What was *the sin* for Peter in this given situation? The sin for Peter was his religious nationalism! Peter and the rest of the disciples were caught up in the old covenant standards regarding Israel, and they struggled to move their minds into the new thing God was doing for ALL NATIONS through his son, Jesus Christ. Before Jesus Christ ascended, he told the disciples to be his witnesses to the uttermost part of the earth, which would have included Gentiles. It takes nearly fifteen years before Peter actually goes to the Gentiles. Why? We see why in Acts 1:6:

> *When they therefore were come together, they asked of him*

[Jesus Christ], *saying, Lord, wilt thou at this time restore again the kingdom to ISRAEL?*

The disciples did not change their focus from Israel to a worldwide ministry focus. Their focus remained Israel, Israel, Israel. Peter's religious nationalism led him to disobey and not fully answer God's call in his life, which was to take this Word to Gentiles. It was this record that taught me a very valuable lesson about our heavenly Father. Why is God so full of grace and mercy? Why is God so long-suffering with us? It is because God cannot violate our free will! God cannot possess us and force us to do anything, including answering His call upon our lives. Therefore, God waited for Peter and was long-suffering with him while Peter grew and developed into the knowledge of taking the Word to the Gentiles.

To assist Peter in his growth, God gave him a dynamic vision to show him once again to move *now* toward the Gentiles (Acts 10:9-20). This extra vision was grace, for God only has to tell us something once for it to be true. The Father telling Peter again to go to the Gentiles was an act of grace. Once Peter understood the vision, he immediately moved. Because Peter and the rest of the disciples did not immediately move toward the Gentiles on the day, Pentecost, God's enemy, the adversary, was almost successful in completely talking the disciples out of their calling.

Here is another great lesson in all of this: do not hesitate in answering your call or goal. When God calls, you answer! When God calls, you get up and move, move, move—or you, like Peter, will run the risk of the adversary stealing and destroying the call. If you move on the call of God, then God will move in your life; God will work with you. As Peter moved toward the Gentiles with the word of God, we see an explosion of outreach that was amazing, something that had not been seen up to that point. If God calls, we must trust that He knows what He is doing and just move!

Once again, what dynamic learning is available to us if we just fully consider the Scriptures in detail. We have learned that there are stages and levels to spiritual growth. We have learned that it will take us laying aside things in our lives to truly answer God's call. We have learned that the sin that holds us back varies from person to person and situation to situation. We have also learned that our heavenly Father is rich in grace and mercy and is long-suffering with us, because He can't violate our free will and must allow us room to grow in order to answer His call on our lives and to overcome to reach our goal.

Chapter Seven

Reflecting Him: Excellence

God is simply awesome. I am so thankful for His wonderful grace, love, and mercy. You could exhaust the English language and still never get close to fully understanding and recognizing the beauty and glory of God. One word that comes to mind when thinking of God that is rarely used is "excellence." Excellence has been defined as that which is exceptional, superior, supreme, sterling, and eminent. Our God is truly all of that and then some, yet the world we live in and its people struggle to see God's supreme and eminent nature and work. In fact, the adversary himself does everything in his power to shroud God's excellent ways. One of the ways that the devil does this is by causing God's people to live far below par, or far below what their heavenly Father has called them to.

I am blessed to have two wonderful children. They are unique to me, individually and collectively. Despite their differences and their varied outlooks on life, they often reflect me as their father (as well as reflect their mother). At times, I observe them and swear I am looking in a mirror. They often have my sense of humor, my facial expressions, my intensity, and many other of my attributes. Though this is special to me, in all honesty it is not dramatically unique. A child should to some degree reflect their parent(s). Would you not agree? We can enter almost any home in the world and see children of all races reflecting their parents on some level.

God's children ought to be a reflection of Him as well. God is excellent, and those who represent Him ought to reflect the excellent nature of the heavenly Father. We should strive to be excellent in every phase and category of our lives, for our heavenly Father has truly called us to a life of excellence.

According as his divine power hath given unto us all things that pertain unto life and godliness, through the knowledge of him that hath called us to glory and virtue. (2 Peter 1:3)

God has called, invited, or summoned us to many different things in life. Two of them are glory and virtue. Glory can be defined as manifested power. God has called us to manifest His power in our lives. In fact, He has called us to manifest His power to the point that it attracts the attention of others. But God did not stop just with us manifesting power; he also called us to something else—virtue. According to Bullinger's *Critical Lexicon and Concordance to the English and Greek New Testament*, the word 'virtue' is defined as "superiority in every respect, excellence of any kind." God has called us to not only manifest His power, which attracts attention, but He has also called us to manifest and demonstrate superiority and excellence! God has imparted to us something so precious and valuable that many people have failed to see it, let alone operate it. By giving us His gift of holy spirit, God has given us what we need to truly manifest power and excellence. Did you catch that? Without God's gift of holy spirit, you and I could never truly manifest His power or demonstrate excellence.

A deeper and more profound truth in all of this is that mediocrity is not of God! Look at the world God has created; nothing about it says mediocrity. Look at the beauty and grand, detailed design of the human body that God created. Consider the number of bones in the human body, the number of cells, and the magnificent design of the human heart. Consider the vastness of the human brain and how it can function. How can you consider all these wonderful things created by God and ever ascribe mediocrity to Him? Yet, due to His children—who are to be a reflection of Him—not living up to what God has called us to and made us, we have caused mediocrity to be ascribed to God. We must change this and not allow it to occur. We must renew our minds to the greatness of God's Word and then go forth in every venue of life manifesting God's power (glory) and showing His excellence. Then and only then can we have our heavenly Father truly delight in us because of the excellence we are showing, which is really His.

Preserve me, O God: for in thee do I put my trust. O my soul, thou hast said unto the Lord, Thou art my Lord; my goodness extendeth not to thee; But to the saints that are in the earth, and to the excellent, in whom is all my delight. (Psalms 16:1-3)

Do you see it? It is right there in black and white for us to read, believe, and live. God's Word says that all of His delight is in the excellence of the earth! As I am excellent at work, God delights in me. As I am excellent in relationships, interacting with others, God delights in me. As I am excellent in forgiveness, excellent in loving others, excellent in ministering to others, God delights in me—and in you as well. I must clarify here that being excellent does not mean one is perfect. It is not available for you or me to be perfect, but it is clearly available for us to manifest God's power (glory) and His virtue or excellence.

By showing excellence in all we do—spiritually, physically, mentally, and in our communication and mannerism—we as God's children are then set apart from the world and its systems. Manifesting God's power and His excellence is really the calling card of the believer in this day and time. This is so vital that you must now consider the revolutionary and prophetic truth summarized in the following words: If God's people do not strive to be excellent in every phase of their lives, they will begin to lose their utility (usefulness) and will become irrelevant in the generation that God has called them to.

Let us look at a record in the Old Testament that speaks loudly to the necessity of being excellent in all we do. We can get a running start on this record by first examining what is said in Hebrews 11:4:

By faith Abel offered unto God a more excellent sacrifice than Cain, by which he obtained witness that he was righteous, God testifying of his gifts: and by it he being dead yet speaketh.

Clearly, from this scripture we see that two brothers offered a sacrifice to God, but Abel's was more excellent than Cain's. Why? We can get the answer by going back to the original record of Cain and Abel in Genesis:

And in the process of time it came to pass, that Cain brought of the fruit of the ground an offering unto the Lord. And Abel, he brought of the firstlings of his flock and of the fat thereof. And the Lord had respect unto Abel and to his offering. But unto Cain and to his offering he had not respect. And Cain was very wroth, and his countenance fell. (Genesis 4:3-5)

There are great keys and depths of understanding in these verses if we just take our time and pay attention to what God is saying and revealing to us in this record. One word in particular begins to truly open this record up for us. Both brothers brought an offering to the Lord. Cain brought of the fruit of the ground and Abel brought of his flock. The difference in their respective offerings is not in fruit versus flock. The ultimate demarcation is revealed by the word *firstlings*. Abel brought to the Lord the first of his flock, which ultimately was his best. The word of God does not say that Cain brought the firstlings of his fruit, but simply that he brought fruit of the ground. This section of the word of God is a real preview to the tithe and what is called first-fruit offering or giving. When giving to God, it must be our best, and it must come from the heart of the person giving. Only when we give our best from the heart can we truly say we are being excellent. Abel gave his best, firstlings, from the heart. Cain gave, but it was not his best. Therefore, God had respect unto Abel and his offering, not Cain's. But hold on—this record reveals even more about Cain, and hence more about our human nature in our giving.

And the Lord said unto Cain, Why art thou wroth? and why is thy countenance fallen? If thou doest well, shalt thou not be accepted? (Genesis 4:6-7)

God asked Cain why he was wroth or angry. Now, the next great truth will be appreciated by those of us who are serious about the word of God and understand its great detailed accuracy. A four-letter word is the key in these verses, and that is the word *well*. 'Well' in the Hebrew is *yatab*. Yatab is defined in *New Wilson's Old Testament Word Studies* as "to do in the best manner, with an extraordinary degree of attention, earnestness, activity, and diligence." In other words, to do well is to do something in the most excellent way. God confronts Cain and says to him that if he had done "excellent," not only would his offering have been accepted, but he would be accepted before God as well. Cain made a free-will choice *not* to give his very best from his heart to God. Wow! Can you see the importance of being excellent, not perfect, before our heavenly Father?

The deeper truth here is that one brother established excellence as his lifestyle, while the other had developed the habit of not giving his best. This truth ought to speak loud volumes into the heart of man. We now live in a world where everyone is trying to cut corners. We live in a world where men have taken their cue from Cain instead of Abel, and as a result, the overall society and world are suffering consequences on so many levels due to men failing to do "well" or that which is excellent. For the believer, excellence is, and must always be, a renewed mind principle. Unless the believer strives to be excellent in all he or she does, they will eventually drift back into the normalcy and mediocrity of the society, community, or environment in which they live. By following the cue of Cain, the believer runs the risk of having their light extinguished, but if the believer takes his lifestyle cue from Abel and does well or excellent in all he or she does, then we can remain the "light of the world" and the "city that is set on an hill" (Matthew 5:14).

Now, to ensure that excellence is not just something we talk about around the kitchen table but is manifested by us daily, I want to show you the links to excellence. The first link is our thoughts. Our minds and thoughts must be brought into harmony with God and His Word. God's Word is perfect and excellent, so as I think His Word, my thoughts can become excellent. This process is called the renewed mind.

And be not conformed to this world: but be ye transformed by the renewing of your mind, that ye may prove what is that good, acceptable, and perfect, will of God. (Romans 12:2)

God declares that His Word, which is His will, is three things: good, acceptable, and perfect. So, I, by my free-will choice, must decide to line up my thinking with God's Word, which is good, acceptable, and perfect. By doing so, I am bringing my mind under subjection to the most excellent thing in the entire world, God's Word. This is the first key or link to getting us to the daily practical reality of excellence. If I break down here and refuse to allow God's thoughts to be my thoughts, I will never be able to reach the other two links, and hence will never truly manifest God's power or excellence.

Finally, brethren, whatsoever things are true, whatsoever things are honest, whatsoever things are just, whatsoever things are pure, whatsoever things are lovely, whatsoever things are of good report; if there be any virtue [excellence], *and if there be any praise, think on these things. (Philippians 4:8)*

What makes God so loving? It's the reality that He has standards. God so loves that He will even provide us direction for our thinking! Earthly parents who will not provide standards and guidelines for their children to follow and mold themselves to are on the verge of being child abusers. We don't let our earthly children make up their own rules for living, we guide them. God is my heavenly Father. Who better to guide my thinking than Him? Hence, God tells us to think on things that are true, honest, just, pure, lovely, of good report, and things that have *excellence* and praise! There is nothing on earth that is more true, honest, just, pure, lovely, of good report, and excellent than God's Word. That is why our thoughts being in alignment with God's Word is the first link to getting us to daily manifestation of His excellence.

The next link for excellence (after our thoughts) is the words we speak. What do we speak or say on a daily basis? What words dominate our daily conversations? What is the focal point of our tongue? Do we think one thing and talk another? We can never be a reflection of God's excellence until we get our thinking and words in harmony. Our words must be directly linked to our thoughts, both positively and negatively. Whatever thoughts we have in abundance in our minds will eventually manifest themselves in our words, speech, and/or confessions. If you think negatively, you will talk negatively. If you think God's Word in abundance (and His Word is excellent), then the words you speak will be excellent.

And my tongue shall speak of thy righteousness and of thy praise all the day long. (Psalms 35:28)

My tongue can't speak of anything that is not in my thinking. To speak of God's righteousness and praise "all the day long," these things must be in my thinking all day long.

You can clearly see the thought-speech link in Proverbs 10:31: "*The mouth of the just bringeth forth wisdom …*" Your mouth brings forth what is in your thinking. The reason anyone can speak wisdom is because wisdom is in their thoughts. Get the word of God in your thoughts in order to have it in your mouth, words, confessions, and conversations.

The final link or step in manifesting God's excellence is *action*. We must take action on the word of God in order for the excellence of God to come forth. I can think the word of God and talk the word of God all day long but never take any action. Hence, all three links must be connected (thoughts-speech-action) to truly bring forth that which God has deposited within us via holy spirit. I can think love and connect that to speech about love, but until I actually take action on love, I have failed to love. The proof of excellence will always be rooted in the three-fold link of thought-speech-action.

As we examine the Scriptures, we see that Jesus Christ understood these principles and mastered them in his daily living. He clearly connected thoughts, speech, and actions and therefore was able to daily bring forth the excellence and power of God. We can see this as we examine a record found in the Gospel of Luke. Jairus, the ruler of the synagogue, came and fell down at Jesus's feet, asking Jesus to come to his home where his only daughter lay dying. Jesus Christ accepted the offer to go, but as he went, something else occurred. As we review this record, I want you to see the dynamic focus and discipline of the mind of Jesus Christ and his ability to shift his mind from one situation to another without becoming overwhelmed or distracted (hint: a distracted or overwhelmed mind can't keep with the pattern of thoughts-speech-action to bring forth God's excellence in a given situation).

And, behold, there came a man named Jairus, and he was ruler of the synagogue: and fell down at Jesus' feet, and besought him that he would come into his house: For he had one only daughter, about twelve years of age, and she lay a dying. But as he went the people thronged him. (Luke 8:41-42)

Jesus always did the will of the Father. The Father's will is to bring healing to all those who believe. Hence, without any real hesitation, Jesus moved to bring forth God's excellence (healing) in this situation. Yet, as he moved, a large crowd gathered and Jesus was being touched and pushed. Jesus Christ could have allowed the crowd to become a distraction to him while going to heal Jairus's daughter, but he maintained his focus and kept moving.

And a woman having an issue of blood twelve years, which had spent all her living upon physicians, neither could be healed of any, came behind him, and touched the border of his garment: and immediately her issue of blood stanched.

And Jesus said, Who touched me? When all denied, Peter and they that were with him said, Master, the multitude throng thee and press thee, and sayest thou, Who touched me?

And Jesus said, Somebody hath touched me: for I perceive that virtue is gone out of me.

And when the woman saw that she was not hid, she came trembling, and falling down before him, she declared unto him before all the people for what cause she had touched him, and how she was healed immediately.

And he said unto her, Daughter, be of good comfort: thy faith hath made thee whole; go in peace. (Luke 8:43-48)

As Jesus Christ moved, having his thoughts, speech, and actions in harmony with the will of God, he was able to bring great deliverance to people, and we can do the same by following his example. As people believe the integrity of the word of God that we live and teach, they can receive God's great healing in their lives, and they can have it without a bunch of fanfare or religious ritual. Jesus Christ did not make this woman do a religious ritual to receive her healing. Her faith (believing), her thought-speech-action link is what led her to be healed, but the record now takes a dramatic change for Jairus.

In Luke 8:49-50, watch how Jesus Christ focused discipline to have his thoughts, speech, and actions in harmony with God, which aided him in helping Jairus do the same and bring great deliverance to Jairus's daughter:

While he yet spake, there cometh one from the ruler of the synagogue's house, saying to him, Thy daughter is dead; trouble not the Master. But when Jesus heard it, he answered him, saying, Fear not: believe only, and she shall be made whole."

Here is real life. At times, things in life can change abruptly or drastically. How we handle our thoughts-speech-actions in these critical moments make all the difference between victory and defeat. Jesus Christ had his mind so locked into the will of God that he refused to allow the environment or circumstances to change his thinking in the situation. He immediately recognized that the dramatic change of events could impact Jairus to the point where he could no longer believe to see his daughter not only healed, but now raised from the dead. Therefore, Jesus Christ responded with a thunderbolt of truth and said, "Fear not." Fear is like acid running loose in one's mind and life. It begins to burn everything it touches, leaving scars and hindering one from truly believing the word of God. Jesus shows Jairus that in life you really only have two choices: fear or believe God and His Word. Fear never brings wholeness to your life, but believing God's Word not only brings wholeness to your life but the lives of others.

And when he came into the house, he suffered [allowed] *no man to go in, save Peter, and James, and John, and the father and mother of the maiden. And all wept, and bewailed her: but he said, Weep not; she is not dead, but sleepeth. (Luke 8:51-52)*

Can you visualize the scene? By the time Jesus and the rest make it to Jairus's house, the news of his only daughter's death had spread through the community, and the community had now gathered at the home. It's clear that Jairus was a beloved member of his community, and the people loved his daughter as well, as demonstrated by them weeping and bewailing her. This word, "bewail," in the Greek carries a strong connotation. It means to grieve to the point of striking one's self, to mourn to the point of striking one's breast. This is deep-seated hurt and pain. Imagine what this type of mourning could do to one's thinking. Imagine how Jesus Christ may have become tempted to quit in his thinking and say, "You are right. She is dead. There's nothing I can do." Yet the master teacher would not allow the grief and mourning of others to infiltrate his mind and break down his thought-speech-action link that allowed him to bring forth the glory and excellence of God in this most heart-wrenching and critical time.

And they laughed him to scorn, knowing that she was dead. And he put them all out, and took her by the hand, and called, saying, Maid, arise. And her spirit came again, and she arose straightway: and he commanded to give her meat. And her parents were astonished: but he charged them that they should tell no man what was done. (Luke 8: 53-56)

What an emotional rollercoaster. One minute, people are grieving so deeply that they begin to strike their breast, and the next moment they are laughing at Jesus Christ to scorn. However, being the great Son of God that he was, Jesus Christ did not let people's praise of him or their criticism of him move him off the word and will of God. He clearly recognized that the people were unable to control their thinking and speech and that their unbelief could eventually impact him. Therefore, he does something on the surface that appears to be unloving and mean-spirited—he put people out of the room. Two things can't occupy the same space. Many times, in life, to get the deliverance we want or need, we need to get rid of things. We need to put things or people out of our lives. As soon as the thing or person who is hindering us is removed, deliverance comes! This is seen clearly in this record. Jesus put out the ones who could not believe that it was God's will for this girl to be delivered, and right on the heels of this comes God's excellence—deliverance! Jairus's daughter was raised from the dead because the Son of God refused to compromise on the word of God in his thoughts, speech, and actions.

Jairus's family was able to see firsthand the reality of the excellence of the heavenly Father manifested by His Son, Jesus Christ.

What a word of God we have, if people only knew. God has given us His gift of holy spirit that we may fully demonstrate His glory and His excellence. By demonstrating His glory and excellence, we can attract the attention of others and introduce them to our loving heavenly Father. God is our Father, and we are to be a reflection of Him. So, go forth from this day forward, reflecting Him to a dark world by showing His excellence in your thoughts, speech, and actions, just like Jesus Christ did.

Chapter Eight

God's Healing Wholeness

Beloved, I wish above all things that thou mayest prosper and be in health, even as thy soul prospereth. (3 John 2)

The word of God is the will of God. What God wants and desires for our lives can be found in the pages of His holy writ, the Scriptures, the word of God. In the above verse, God clearly tells us that He desires that each one of us prosper and be in good health. God wants us to prosper in every phase and category of our lives. He wants me to prosper mentally, physically, emotionally, spiritually, and yes financially, but to truly have godly prosperity and enjoy it, we must have the accompanying health to go with it. Hence, God not only wants us to prosper, but He wants us to have health, physical wholeness, to go with it. What good is it to prosper financially but be sickly your whole life and not be able to truly enjoy the prosperity the heavenly Father has provided? The flip side of the equation is also true, but so many Christians fail to see it. God never intended for me to have great health, wholeness, and then be poverty stricken. God's true and ultimate will is that His children have both physical wholeness and material/

financial prosperity.

In this teaching, I want to show you, up close, four aspects or teaching points of God's healing wholeness, and they are:

1. Healing is a large part of God's nature
2. Healing is more than physical
3. Healing requires believing from the person seeking healing
4. God's disciples are to bring God's healing to their communities

Healing Is a Large Part of God's Nature

There are many aspects to God's nature. He is a God of joy, peace, and comfort. He is a God that provides and protects. The one aspect of His nature that is frequently overlooked is that God heals. This part of God's nature has been shrouded and cloaked by devilish teaching by so-called men and women of God who blame God for death and teach that God allows sickness to come into your life to make you humble. God never allows evil in to bring about good. God truly can bring good out of evil, but He does not allow evil to happen to produce good. The devil is the author, origin, and source of every evil on the planet, including sickness. When the devil in the garden of Eden tricked and deceived Adam and Eve to sin and break fellowship with God, their sin opened the world to a life of sin and sickness, and God has been moving to bring wholeness to humanity ever since. It is interesting to see that another word for healing is *restore* or *restoration*.

We see God moving to bring healing and restoration to

the entire earth in Genesis 1:

In the beginning God created the heaven and earth. And the earth was without form, and void; and darkness was upon the face of the deep. And the spirit of God moved upon the face of the waters. And God said, Let there be light … (Genesis 1:1-3)

As we examine these verses, we need to ask questions to see the deeper and bigger meaning behind the surface. In verse 2, it says "and the earth was without form." Based on verse 1 telling us that God created the heaven and earth, it would appear that God created it without form, made it void, and placed darkness on the earth. This is not the truth, and one word in verse 2 is the key to understanding this. In Hebrew, there is no such word as "was." The Hebrew equivalent is the word or phrase *became* or *to become*. In other words, God did not create the heaven and earth to be without form, void, or with darkness on it. The earth became this way. Something happened between verse 1and verse 2 that led the earth to become without form, void, and to become dark. If we examine the word of God and study it properly, we find out what actually happened between verses 1 and 2.

And there appeared a great wonder in heaven; a woman clothed with the sun, and the moon under her feet, and upon her head a crown of twelve stars: And she being with child cried, travailing in birth, and pained to be delivered. And there appeared another wonder in heaven; and behold a great red dragon, having seven heads and ten horns, and seven crowns upon his heads. And his tail drew a third part of the stars of heaven, and did cast them to the earth … (Revelation 12:1-4)

The red dragon is the devil. There was war in heaven before man was created on the earth. The archangel Michael fought with Lucifer and kicked him out of heaven (Revelation 12:9), along with the other angels who rebelled with him (the term "star" is often symbolic language in the Scriptures for angels). Once cast out of heaven, the word of God says they were cast out into the earth. Once casted to the earth, Lucifer, now called the devil, Satan (red dragon), along with the fallen angels, racked and ruined the earth. This is how we get to without form, void, and darkness upon the earth in Genesis 1:2.

Now, watch our wonderful God go to work in Genesis. Everything God does from Genesis 1:2 is to heal or restore the earth after what Lucifer did. So, in Genesis 1:2 we see the spirit of God "moved." Why did the spirit of God move? To heal and restore the earth so that He could place His creations on it—man and woman. Isn't that amazing? One of God's first acts is to heal. This is why I say that a large part of God's nature is healing.

We can also see a large part of God's healing nature in the life of his son, Jesus Christ:

I always do those things that please him. (John 8:29)

because I seek not mine own will, but the will of the Father which hath sent me. (John 5:30)

For I came down from heaven, not to do mine own will, but the will of him that sent me. (John 5:38)

Jesus Christ declares that he came not to the earth to do

his own will but the will of the Father. He declares that he always does those things that please the Father. So, when Jesus Christ moved among the people and brought healing, whose will was he doing? He was doing the Father's will. When Jesus Christ raised men/women from the dead, he was demonstrating the will of the Father. When Jesus Christ healed lepers, he was exhibiting the will of the Father. When Jesus Christ gave sight to a man born blind, that was the will of the Father. Can you not see that part of God's nature is healing?

In case you still don't see it, let me show you another truth that is fantastic. Here are the chapters in the books of Matthew through John that have healing records:

- Matthew: chapters 8, 9, 12, 14, 15, 17, 19, 21
- Mark: chapters 1, 2, 3, 5, 6, 7, 8, 9, 10
- Luke: chapters 4, 5, 6, 7, 8, 9, 14
- John: chapters 4, 5, 9, 11

Healing Is More Than Physical

God's will is that we have physical wholeness, but that is not all of His will. Something that is broken needs to be healed; it needs to be restored. Clearly, man and woman in this walk of life are not only physically hurt or broken. We can have broken thoughts, broken emotions, and be broken spiritually. God's will and nature is to bring His healing wholeness to every category of our lives. A person who has not received the new birth (Romans 10:9,10) is broken spiritually. God makes it available for that person to be healed spiritually via the new birth. If our emotions are broken or out of order, God makes it available for us to be healed in this category as well. God does not just save us spiritually or physically. He desires to save us to the uttermost through the work of his dear Son, Jesus Christ.

> *But this man* [Jesus Christ], *because he continueth ever, hath an unchangeable priesthood. Wherefore he is able also to save them to the uttermost that come unto God by him, seeing he ever liveth to make intercession for them. (Hebrews 7:24-25)*

God's word says that any man or woman who comes to God via Jesus Christ can be saved to the uttermost. So, we see that God's healing wholeness is more than just physical. God can bring His healing wholeness to every category of your life, to every crevice of your mind, to every joint and organ of your body, and to every emotional scar you have ever had. This is saving one to the uttermost.

Healing Requires Believing from the Person Seeking Healing

In order for God to heal me, I must believe that He can. I must be fully persuaded in my mind that God's will is to heal me of any sickness, including sicknesses that are spiritual, mental, emotional, or physical. Every record in the Bible on healing demonstrates that the person seeking healing showed that they believed God could heal them by the actions they took. There are only three categories of people who God does not demand believing from to get healed:

1. Children too young to believe or to understand what believing is. In their case, God then demands that

their parent(s) believe for their child's healing. This is seen in the record in the Mark 9:16-23, where Jesus Christ tells a father who is seeking deliverance for his son who has a dumb spirit, "*If thou canst believe ...*" The child was unable to believe due to his condition, so his father had to believe for his son's healing.

2. A person who, according to the medical field, is deranged. In their case, the person who is ministering healing is required to believe God for the person's healing. This can be seen in the record of Matthew 8:28-34, where Jesus Christ meets two men coming out of the tombs who were possessed (in our day and time the medical field would call these men mentally deranged). Jesus Christ does the believing while ministering and casting out the devils. Nowhere in the record do you see either possessed man do any believing to be healed.
3. A person who is dead. Then the one ministering healing (raising them from the dead, which is a miracle) has to do the believing. You see this clearly shown in John 11:41-44, where Jesus Christ raises Lazarus from the dead. Lazarus is dead. He can't believe in God to raise him from the dead. You also see in the record that the sisters of Lazarus did not believe either, so Jesus Christ was fully persuaded of the will of God and did the believing to get Lazarus raised from the dead.

What doth it profit, my brethren, though a man say he hath faith, and not have works? Can faith save him? (James 2:14)
Even so faith, if it hath not works, is dead, being alone.

(James 2:17)

But wilt thou know, O vain man, that faith without works is dead? (James 2:20)

The word *dead* in this section of Scripture is defined as destitute of power, inactive. I can say I have faith, but until I literally take action in the body/soul category, my so-called faith is dead, destitute of power and inactive. Action is required of the person seeking God's healing. The woman in the gospels with the bloody issue had to take action to get her healing. She got up from where she was, pushed her way through the crowd, touched the hem of Jesus Christ's garment, and was delivered. This would have never happened if she would have just stayed at home hoping and wishing to get healed. She made her faith alive. She made sure it was not dead, destitute of power and inactive by literally taking the necessary action to get healed. The blind man had to take action on the words of Jesus Christ and go wash in the pool. His healing did not come until he took action as Jesus Christ commanded (John 9:5-7).

God's Disciples Are to Bring God's Healing to Their Communities

Are you a disciple? Then you have been authorized by God and His Son to bring God's healing wholeness to your community. Just like the records of Matthew-John are loaded with examples of Jesus Christ bringing God's healing wholeness. The book of Acts is loaded with the disciples of the first century church bringing God's healing wholeness to their communities. Physical healing is mentioned in almost every section of Acts (with the exception of Acts 11:22 and 12:24).

The book of Acts records the rise and expansion of the first-century church. In the Gospels, you see Jesus Christ walking with power to heal, but once the day of Pentecost comes in Acts 2, you see the disciples moving as Jesus Christ did to bring healing where they went and to their local communities. The disciples of the first-century church show us that it is still God's will to heal, and that it is God's will that we partner with Him to bring healing in our day and time.

And believers were the more added to the Lord, multitudes both of men and women. Insomuch that they brought forth the sick into the streets, and laid them on beds and couches, that at least the shadow of Peter passing by might overshadow some of them. There came also a multitude out of the cities round about unto Jerusalem, bringing sick folks, and them which were vexed with unclean spirits: and they were healed every one. (Acts 5:14-16)

Can you imagine the joy in those cities? Can you imagine the joy of the individuals who got healed? What about the joy and relief of their families? Imagine not being able to walk, and then in one day you are healed in the name of Jesus Christ and able to walk. Imagine being bedridden, the financial cost to a family, and the emotional hurt to the individual and their family. Peter and the other disciples brought the healing power of God to their communities and demonstrated that it is God's will to heal to the uttermost.

And it came to pass, as Peter passed throughout all quarters, he came down also to the saints which dwelt at Lydda. And there he found a certain man named Aeneas, which had kept his bed eight years, and was sick of palsy. And Peter said unto him, Aeneas, Jesus Christ maketh thee whole: arise, and make thy bed. And he arose immediately. And all that dwelt at Lydda and Saron saw him, and turned to the Lord. (Acts 9:32-35)

This word of God excites me so much that my skin is tingling as I write this. These few verses are loaded with so much wisdom and learning. Notice it says Peter "found" this man. This means Peter was looking. You hardly ever find anything that you are not actively looking for. Peter found Aeneas. He did not stumble into him; Peter found him. Peter was actively looking for someone to share the word of God with. He was actively looking for someone to bring God's healing wholeness to. What a great lesson. As we look for people with needs and hungry hearts with the great heart of service that Peter had, God will open doors for us to find those hungry hearts, those individuals and families who need God's healing; they are out there.

Jesus Christ declared in his day: "*The harvest truly is great, but the labourers are few: pray ye therefore the lord of the harvest, that he would send forth labourers into his harvest*" (Luke 10:2). This bold statement of truth by Jesus Christ is still true today. In this record in Acts 9, we see a laborer named Peter in the harvest bringing God's great healing wholeness. Not only did Peter bring wholeness to Aeneas, this wholeness was seen by others and brought tremendous impact to their lives. The impact of *one* disciple bringing God's healing wholeness to *one* man caused two cities to turn to the Lord.

You and I must see ourselves like Peter. We must see ourselves as being authorized by God to bring healing. We must see that healing can open great doors to win others to the Lord. If Peter could make an impact on two cities in his day, we have to be able to at least make an impact on our local neighborhood and community. We as disciples must renew our minds to the word of God to recognize who we are in Christ. We must see that we are truly in Christ's stead (2 Corinthians 5:20) and have the authority and authorization from God Himself to reconcile men and women to God and bring healing, which is part of the reconciliation process.

It is God's will to heal. Healing is part of His nature. Healing is more than just physical, and God's will is to heal us to the uttermost. Healing requires action, believing on the part of the one seeking healing. Then, when you have received the new birth, you are authorized by God himself to partner with Him and bring that uttermost healing to our communities in the powerful name of Our Lord Jesus Christ. God's healing wholeness is yours and for you to share with others, so get it and share it!

Chapter Nine

The Love of God, Part One

"Charity [love, the love of God] *never faileth ..." (1 Corinthians 13:8)*

God's Word boldly declares that love never fails. Do we truly believe this? If love never fails, that means there is no power on earth that can rule or dominate love. No governmental power can dominate love. No nuclear bomb can rule or dominate love, for love is the most powerful force on the earth. However, few people believe this truth, and most shamefully some Christian believers do not believe it either. One Bible translation I found used the word "falleth" instead of "faileth." Isn't that amazing? Love will never fail or fall. Hence, if I truly walk with the love of God in my heart and life, that means I can't fall or fail. Can you see how big this issue of love is, and can you see why the devil works overtime to ensure that people never understand what love is and that they never believe in it and walk in it? But hold on—it gets bigger and better.

When I was a child, I spake as a child, I understood as a child, I thought as a child: but when I became a man, I put away childish things. (1 Corinthians 13:11)

I have often heard this verse quoted over the years, but usually out of its proper context. What is the context of 1 Corinthians 13 about? It is about the love of God. So, when Paul says he became a man, it means that he was only able to become a real man by walking in the love of God. That's right—you can't become a real spiritual, godly man or woman without walking in the love of God. In fact, the context tells us that anything outside the love of God must be considered "childish," and can I add "uncivilized." However, people frequently treat love as if it is something they fell over and into. They treat love as if it is the newfound flu and they have "caught" it. Love is not something you fall into or catch. Love for the believer is, and must be, an intentional, on-purpose action! You must will to love, and this is where most people fall short, especially when something arises that is negative and challenges their will. Yet, we all claim to love the man Christ Jesus who loved all of us enough to die for us.

Was Jesus Christ's will challenged? You bet your life it was challenged, yet his love for God and for us was bigger than the challenge of death he faced. He has left us a faultless and perfect example of what it means to truly love God and others. Jesus Christ loved intentionally and on purpose. At the end of 1 Corinthians 13, Paul tells us of three great realities: faith (believing), hope, and charity (love). Out of these three great realities of life, Paul says that the greatest reality is love. Love is greater than faith and hope. What a revelation to my heart to understand this. I grew up in a denominational church where I heard minister after minister tell the members that if they just had more faith, their lives would be better. This is not true because the greatest reality in life is love, not faith.

For in Jesus Christ neither circumcision availeth any thing nor uncircumcision; but faith which worketh by love. (Galatians 5:6)

The word 'worketh' is translated to *energo* in Greek, which can be defined as to be active, efficient, fervent, energized. The love of God activates and energizes our believing, our faith. Without the love of God in my heart and life, my believing can't be energized, activated, or stirred by God. So, when all the old preachers were saying you just need "more faith," they were not accurate. What Christians need is more love! Christianity does not have a faith problem; Christianity has a love problem. In fact, I will be so bold to say that nothing in the word of God will truly work for you if done or operated outside the love of God.

We are born again and now have holy spirit, but holy spirit can't truly work the way God has designed it if we are living our lives outside the love of God. We have been given authorization to utilize the name of Jesus Christ in this walk, but the name of Jesus Christ can't work properly outside the love of God. If it could, then the name of Jesus Christ is no better than saying "open sesame." Without the love of God in my heart and life, I will continue to come up short. So, the ultimate challenge to the Christian believer is not to have more faith. The ultimate challenge for the believer is to *love bigger*! By loving God bigger, my believing and/or faith then can truly grow.

Love comes from God, who is spirit. Therefore, love is spiritual and does not come from man's reasoning ability. Man can never reason himself into the love of God, but certainly can and does reason himself *out* of the love of God. The love of God is not based on a feeling, emotion, or event. Your love for God must be based and rooted in an unshaken commitment to God and His Word. This is why in our quest for spiritual maturity, we must never forget the main ingredient to spiritual maturity, the love of and for God. This love of God must be on display, and it must be displayed in how we treat one another.

Ye have heard that it hath been said, Thou shalt love thy neighbor and hate your enemy. But I say unto you, Love your enemies, bless them that curse you, do good to them that hate you, and pray for them which despitefully use you, and persecute you." (Matthew 5:43-44)

You can clearly see that our love of God is to be on display to all. Our love of God is to be manifested to those who love us and even to those who hate us, curse us, and use us. Your love of God is never to be just to and for you.

A new commandment I give unto you, that ye love one another; as I have loved you, that ye also love one another. By this shall all men know that ye are my disciples, if ye love one to another." (John 13:34-35)

In these verses, the great Greek word for love is *agape*. The great theologian E. W. Kenyon noted in his work that the word 'agape' did not appear in any classical Greek literature until after the coming of Jesus Christ. Prior to that, Greek literature utilized two words for the term love: *eros* and *phileo.* Eros was used for love shown by animals and was based on instinct. We get our English word 'erotic' from the Greek word eros. Phileo was used to describe brotherly love, love that was based on conditions, like "you scratch my back, I'll scratch yours." The word 'Philadelphia' comes from phileo. Hence, the city Philadelphia is known as the "City of Brotherly Love."

Agape is completely different from eros and phileo. It used to describe the highest form of love available to man. It is love that is based on God and the principles of God's word. It is not love based on an erotic feeling or a condition. It is love that does not love *because* of, but love that loves *despite* of. You can see where eros and phileo fall extremely short of the love Jesus Christ was talking about and made available to the born-again believer. If I have eros, or erotic love, then I will only love when that erotic feeling comes upon me. If the feeling is not there, then I can't love. If I have phileo, then I can only love if the conditions are right or met. I can't love you unless you do for me first.

Neither of these kinds of love were demonstrated in the life of Jesus Christ. Do you think Jesus Christ loved strictly based on feelings? Do you think He felt like being tortured, humiliated, and executed? Do you think Jesus Christ died because of the right conditions or because we loved him first? Absolutely not! He died based on spiritual principles, based on the word of God, his love for God, and his love for his fellow man. Jesus Christ died based on agape love.

Love [agape] *worketh no ill to his neighbor: therefore love is the fulfilling of the law. (Romans 13:10)*

Love will never allow one to bring evil to his neighbor. A man who walks in love does not need law. Why? When walking according to the standard of the love of God, a person is walking in the highest law available to man, the law of love. As we walk in the love of God, we fulfill the law. Jesus Christ synthesized this when he declared that all the previous laws of Moses were really melted down into two laws: (1) to love God with all thy heart, soul, mind, and strength, and (2) to love your neighbor as thyself (Matthew 22:36-40, Mark 12:29-31).

Another great key to truly understanding the love of God is to understand that walking in love is *not* based on convenience. It is really easy to love when all the conditions are right or perfect. It is easy to say you love God or a person when it costs you nothing, but when the wind of life changes direction and brings in the cold front of the adversary, how easy is it to love then? Oftentimes in life, challenges will reveal how deep your love for God really goes. When the sun is shining and you don't have a care in the world, everybody has this deep love for God. Let us take a look at one of the parables of Jesus Christ to fully show and demonstrate my point that love is not based on convenience:

And Jesus answering said, A certain man went down from Jerusalem to Jericho, and fell among thieves, which stripped him of his raiment, and wounded him, and departed, leaving him half dead. And by chance there came down a certain priest that way: and when he saw him, he passed by on the other side.

And likewise a Levite, when he was at the place, came and looked on him, and passed by on the other side. But a certain Samaritan, as he journeyed, came where he was: and when he saw him, he had compassion on him, and went to him, and bound up his wounds, pouring in oil and wine, and set him on his own beast, and brought him to an inn, and took care of him.

And on the morrow when he departed, he took out two pence, and gave them to the host, and said unto him, Take care of him; and whatsoever thou spendest more, when I come again, I will repay thee.

Which now of these three, thinkest thou, was neighbor unto him that fell among thieves? And he said, He that shewed mercy on him. Then said Jesus unto him, Go, and do thou likewise. (Luke 10:30-37)

Jesus Christ, the master teacher of God's Word, utilizes this parable to teach so many wonderful truths and to reveal what a true heart of love for God and man looks like. To fully appreciate this record, we need to look at some background information. I have never been to Jerusalem, but I have been told by others who have been there, and via my own personal study of the area, that the road from Jerusalem to Jericho was unique. This area has been described as mostly downhill travel, with roads that twist and turn and have mountains on either side. This area would be a great area for potential thieves to hide out and await their next victim. Now, notice the two men that Jesus Christ says passed by the man who was wounded were a priest and a Levite. Here are two people with religious background and pedigree, yet they do not stop to help this man. The powerful lesson here is that religion never has real love in it. Religion is nothing but a system of ritual where men and women make sense knowledge attempts to come to know the one True God. Unfortunately, in our day and time, there is lots of religion in Christianity.

Let me tell you why I think the priest and the Levite passed by. One reason was fear. They understood the potential danger of the road from Jerusalem to Jericho. They probably thought this wounded man was part of some elaborate hoax to hurt them. You see, fear will always make men and women selfish and cowardly. The moment the priest and Levite began to think of themselves above everything else, they walked right out of the love of God. The moment they allowed the conditions to push their minds and emotions into the concern of if it was convenient to help this man, they walked right out of love. As I said earlier in this teaching, man can never reason himself into the love of God, but he certainly can reason himself out of it, and that is exactly what the priest and Levite did.

Thank God Jesus Christ did not end the teaching with the priest and Levite. Along came the Samaritan, with limited religious background and no religious pedigree in this particular culture. Jesus Christ declares that the Samaritan was moved by compassion. Trace where the Samaritan's compassion came from and you will run smack into *love*. Love led to his compassion, and compassion led to him taking action to help this wounded man. When the religious priest and Levite saw the man, they quickly considered what would happen to them if they helped this man. However, the Samaritan considered what would happen to the man if he did not help him. What a mindset of love!

What a parable of truth that Jesus Christ taught. Jesus Christ closed the parable by telling the man to go forth and show mercy like the Samaritan. God's mercy toward any of us is always rooted in love. Therefore, when he said to go and show mercy, he was also saying to go and show love!

When God saw you dead in trespasses and sins, He did not ask what would happen to Him if he helped you. He asked what would happen to *you* if He did not help you. Therefore, God, out of love, sent his Son to redeem us from our fall. Jesus Christ followed the loving example of His heavenly Father and did what he had to do in order to redeem us, being more concerned about us then he was himself. Do you think it was convenient for Jesus Christ to die for us? Do you think on the day of his crucifixion that God woke His Son up that morning and said, "Good morning, Jesus. The weather is perfect, and this is a great day for you to be tortured and crucified for the sins of the world. It is a convenient day for you to be beaten, mocked, tortured, and dragged through the streets like a common criminal and be publicly executed"? There was nothing convenient about it, yet Jesus Christ's love for God and his love for us motivated him to get the job done. What a man, what a messiah, what a friend! Now we must follow his example and love enough—even when it is not convenient—to reconcile man back to God. This is our charge, this is our duty, this is our privilege, to love as God and His Son loved.

In the closing of his book *The New Kind of Love*, the great theologian E. W. Kenyon writes "Every thought, every motive, every act outside of love dwarfs us, binds us, holds us in bondage, keeps us from our best. Every love act enriches us. Every love thought makes us better. We think love, and then we act love … you see, love is revolutionary; it is not commonplace … it takes a common man and makes him uncommon."

Let us continue in love and become those uncommon men and women that follow the example of the Master (Jesus Christ) and his disciples and turn this world upside down with love.

Chapter Ten

Love of God, Part Two

From our previous teaching, we have seen that there are three great realities in life for the Christian believer: faith, hope, and charity (1Corinthians 13:13). We have also learned that the greatest of these is *love*. Love of God is the main ingredient in our spiritual growth process. Love is so big and dynamic that Jesus Christ shows us that we can love God on four levels.

And thou shalt love the Lord thy God with all thy heart, and with all thy soul, and with all thy mind, and with all thy strength: this is the first commandment. (Mark 12:30)

Jesus Christ shows us here that if a person truly wants to love God, it is a necessity to love God on four levels: heart, soul, mind, and strength. (Even though these four levels of love are not the focus or purpose of this teaching, what a great piece of research for us to consider in the future.) We also learned from E. W. Kenyon that the love of God is what makes a common man an uncommon man and gives him courage and allows him to be fearless. If we as Christians want to be truly set apart from the world, it is going to take us manifesting this love of God on a horizontal basis to others. It is important for the believer to have accurate knowledge of God's Word, but knowledge of God's Word alone will not get the job done.

In John 13:35, Jesus Christ boldly declared that love is what would let the world know that we are his disciples, not just knowledge of God's Word. Apostle Paul later pens, via revelation in 1 Corinthians 8, that knowledge of the word of God can "puffeth" up some people, but charity "edifieth." Over and over again, we see God emphasizing in His Word the importance of love. So, with this teaching, I want to show you the reader a little deeper what love is, the attributes of the love of God, and then I will close this teaching by showing how to avoid some of the world's clichés regarding love.

According to Apostle Paul in 1 Corinthians 13:8, he states: "*Charity never faileth …*" Therefore, a Christian can never fail if he or she is truly walking in the love of God. We as believers only fail when we fail to love. In Ephesians 5:2, Paul gives us a deeper look into love:

> *And walk in love, as Christ also hath loved us, and hath given himself for us an offering and a sacrifice to God for a sweetsmelling savour.*

Whenever someone is walking and attempting to duplicate something they have seen in the word of God, they will need some type of pattern to follow. When it comes to walking in the love of God, Paul informs us that Christ is the object of our imitation. If we truly desire to walk in love, then we must follow or imitate the walk of Jesus Christ.

What was the focal point in the love life of Jesus Christ? It was that he gave himself; he sacrificed himself. Giving is always a primary feature in love. Jesus Christ gave himself without hesitance, without reservation or promise of return. There was no "me-ism" or "I-ism" in the walk of Jesus Christ. His daily spiritual and mental focus in life was on how to please the Father and giving to bless others. Jesus Christ understood more than any other human that we can impact others by our lives.

Love is a transcending force. It has the power to not only affect my life but the lives of others. If I choose not to walk in love, that affects more than just me. Our lives are the story of the pebble in the lake. As the pebble strikes the water, it has a ripple effect. Our lives have an impact on others, positive or negative. We choose which impact we will have. The bigger I love, the bigger the ripple effect in life I can have. The smaller or less I love, my life becomes like that smooth stone gliding over the water of life with very little impact. Most people I know want to have a positive impact. Most of us dream of a life where we do great, important things. Our wildest dreams can become reality as we make the choice to walk in the love of God, with Jesus Christ's life being the object of our imitation.

This walking in love is not based on convenience. This walk of love can only really be carried out by those who are committed to the heavenly Father and who demonstrate courage. Let us look at 1 Corinthians 13:4 and see more clearly why love is not based on convenience:

Charity suffereth long, and is kind; charity envieth not; charity vaunteth not itself, is not puffed up.

How easy is it to endure (suffer long)? How convenient is it to suffereth long with other people and situations in life? Yet this is exactly what the love of God does for us and with us. The above verse also says that love is kind. This word, "kind," means to be gentle in spite of ingratitude. It is not always easy or convenient to be kind despite how others are treating you, is it? Yet kindness is an attribute or characteristic of the love of God. Love envieth not, according to the Scriptures. Envy is to be zealous toward or against one. It is to be jealous over the success of another person. Love vaunteth not itself. Vaunteth is to boast or brag. It also means that a person looks to be served versus serving others. This vaunting leads one to be "puffed up." Jesus Christ shows us his humility and his true motive of heart for service in Matthew 20. Remember, Jesus Christ is the object of our imitation in walking in love, so try this one on for size:

Even as the Son of Man came not to be ministered unto, but to minister, and to give his life a ransom for many. (Matthew 20:28)

Now let us go back to 1 Corinthians and examine some additional characteristics of love:

Doth not behave itself unseemly, seeketh not her own, is not easily provoked, thinketh no evil. (1 Corinthians 13:5)

If I am walking in the love of God, I will have corresponding actions or behaviors that are indicative of love. I will not behave unseemly (have poor conduct). If I am walking in the love of God, I will not be seeking to have my way but seeking that which is pleasing to my heavenly Father and will bless others. If I am walking in the love of God, I will not be easily provoked or angered. Many people have short fuses because they lack love. People are easily angered because they lack love in their thinking and hearts. Wow, look at the final characteristic of verse 5! If I am walking in love, I am thinking no evil. God has allowed us the ability to gauge our love walk by examining our thinking. If I am thinking evil, or the end result, conclusion, or fruit of my thinking is evil, then I am not walking in love.

Now you must ask yourself the question, who determines what is evil? Simple answer—God determines what is evil, not me or you. Hence, my walk in love must begin with having my thinking in alignment with what God determines is good. As a result of doing this, my actions will come in harmony with this walk of love. Too many times in life we spend all of our energy trying to fix or change our behavior, when the real key to change, the real key to love, is our thought life. Change your thinking and you can change your behavior because behavior follows mindset.

Well, you may be saying now, "All this love talk is good, but there are some folks I just don't like. Can't I love people and not like them?" In life, we must beware of what I call worldly clichés. Our challenge is to bring every thought "captive" to the obedience of Christ (2 Corinthians 10:5). We are to bring every thought to the light of God's Word to determine if it is a true godly thought or not. Remember what I said earlier: Jesus Christ is the object of our imitation. So, in light of liking or disliking someone, we need to examine the Scriptures pertaining to Jesus Christ. As we study the Scriptures, we quickly come to the realization that Jesus Christ never dealt with anyone on the basis of like versus dislike. He dealt with people on the basis of love and/or light versus darkness. The two examples in Scripture that immediately come to my mind are the records of Zacchaeus the tax collector in Luke 19 and the woman of Samaria who came to the well at the time Jesus Christ was there.

Zacchaeus was a tax collector. A tax collector in the time of Jesus Christ was an unfavorable occupation. Many people in this time period hated tax collectors or at the very least disliked them. This particular tax collector desired to see Jesus Christ for himself and showed his humility by climbing into a sycamore tree (to do so was a sign of humility, biblically) to get a look at Him. Not only did Zacchaeus get a look at Jesus Christ, but Jesus requested to abide at Zacchaeus's house, which stirred controversy (Luke 19:7). Jesus Christ did not deal with Zacchaeus from the perspective of like or dislike; he dealt with him from the perspective of the love of God. Despite the cultural norm of the day to despise or dislike a person based on their particular occupation (a form of prejudice), Jesus Christ chose to walk in love toward this man and bring salvation to his house, which meant him, his family, and any servants he may have had (Luke 19:9).

Then we see Jesus Christ breaking from the cultural norm of his day again, not dealing with people on the basis of like or dislike, but on the basis of love in John 4. Jesus and his disciples had been on a long teaching/preaching itinerary. Jesus was tired and wanted food and water, so he decided to rest at a well while he sent his disciples off to get meat/food. While at the well, a Samaritan woman came to draw water. Jesus requested that the woman draw water for him as well. This simple act of initiating a conversation with this Samaritan woman arrested her attention. Jesus Christ was a Judean (Jew), and Judeans had nothing to do with Samaritans. In fact, Judeans considered Samaritans to be dogs. Yet despite the cultural and religious differences, despite the norm and tradition of Judeans despising Samaritans, Jesus Christ broke from all of that junk. Why? By now you must know the answer—love! Love motivated Jesus Christ to break from tradition and centuries of prejudice and racism to bring salvation to one woman, who happened to be of the wrong culture. This awesome display of the power of love not only struck the heart of this one woman, but it opened a door into a Samaritan city where Jesus Christ would abide for two days preaching and teaching the word of God (John 4:39-43).

Look at the impact of love. In these two records, Jesus had a choice, to either walk by his emotions, which is really what like or disliking is about, it is your emotions making a choice, or by the love of God. Jesus Christ chose to walk by love, and this choice had a reverberating impact in his day and time. You and I, as followers of the Lord Jesus Christ, are faced with the same exact choice of our master, to either walk by our emotions or walk by the love of God. If we walk by the love of God, we will not fail. If we walk by our emotions, we increase significantly the probability of failure. It takes courage to walk in the love of God. It took courage for Jesus Christ to break from the cultural norms, traditions, and prejudices of his day to go to the house of a tax collector. It took courage for him to speak to a woman, but even more courage to speak to a woman who was considered to be the least in a society. It certainly took courage and fortitude to love enough to be crucified for the sins of the world.

For when we were yet without strength, in due time Christ died for the ungodly. For scarcely for a righteous man will one die: yet peradventure for a good man some would even dare to die. But God commendeth [favorably introduced] his love toward us, in that, while we were yet sinners, Christ died for us. (Romans 5:6-8)

Jesus Christ died for us, the ungodly the sinner. What would lead a man to do such a thing? You got it—love. The love of God burned in the heart of Jesus Christ to the point that it burned to a crisp any aspect of selfishness he could have had. The love of God can and will do the same for you and me. According to Romans 5, God utilized the death of His Son to commend, or favorably introduce, His love to us. What a remarkable reality. Some people believe that the crucifixion of Jesus Christ is the end-all example of love, but God says it was just the beginning of His love; it was His way to favorably introduce agape love to the world. Have you noticed that when you read a book it usually has a section called the introduction? The introduction of a book never tells you the full story or every detail of the book, but it can give you great highlights and coming events. To get the fullness of the book, you have to read it in its entirety. So it is with the love of God. The crucifixion of Jesus Christ is the introduction to God's love. You will have to stay faithful to and with the Father to get the rest of the love He has in store for you. Even then, you still are not able to fully comprehend what God has in store for us who love Him, so say recite 1 Corinthians 2:9:

But as it is written, Eye hath not seen, nor ear heard, neither have entered into the heart of man, the things which God hath prepared for them that LOVE HIM.

May we forever take grasp of God's hand and walk with Him. May we forever remain committed to walking in the love of God and never allow selfishness to dethrone God's love in our hearts. May we keep our eyes on the Lord Jesus Christ, who is the object of our imitation, and may we never allow the stale traditions, cultural norms, and prejudices of our day sway us from this clear path of love that our Lord Jesus Christ has blazed for us.

References

The Holy Bible, King James version.

Bullinger, E. W. *Critical Lexicon and Concordance to the English and Greek New Testament.* Grand Rapids, Michigan: Zondervan Publishing House, 1975.

Kenyon, E. W. *The New Kind of Love.* Kenyon's Publishing Society, 2000.

Rodale, J. I. *The Synonym Finder.* New York: Warner Books Inc., 1986.

Wilson, William. *New Wilson's Old Testament Word Studies.* Grand Rapids, Michigan: Kregel Publications, 1987.

Twitter: Don Smith@V4Truth

Facebook: Facebook.com/don.smith.3950

YouTube Channel: Valiant for Truth

Review Requested:
If you loved this book, would you please provide a review at Amazon.com?

Milton Keynes UK
Ingram Content Group UK Ltd.
UKHW011853161123
432711UK00001B/98

9 781950 015825